JAMIROQUAI

Books LLC®, Reference Series, Memphis, USA, 2011. www.booksllc.net. Copyright: http://creativecommons.org/licenses/by-sa/3.0/deed.en

Table of Contents

Jamiroquai
Jamiroquai... 1
Jamiroquai concerts 4
Jamiroquai discography 5
Jay Kay... 5
Space Clav 6

Jamiroquai albums
1999 Remixes...................................... 7
A Funk Odyssey.................................. 7
Dynamite (Jamiroquai album) 8
Emergency on Planet Earth................. 9
High Times: Singles 1992–2006......... 9
In Store Jam 11
Jay's Selection 11
Late Night Tales: Jamiroquai........... 11
Multiquai... 11
Rock Dust Light Star 12
Synkronized 13
The Return of the Space Cowboy 13
Travelling Without Moving 14

Jamiroquai members
John Thirkell 15
Matt Johnson (keyboardist)............... 16
Mike Smith (saxophonist)................. 17
Nick Fyffe 17
Stuart Zender..................................... 17
Toby Smith.. 18

Jamiroquai songs
(Don't) Give Hate a Chance.............. 19
Alright (Jamiroquai song) 19
An Online Odyssey 19
Blow Your Mind (Jamiroquai song) . 19
Blue Skies (Jamiroquai song) 20
Canned Heat (song)........................... 20
Corner of the Earth............................ 21
Cosmic Girl 21
Deeper Underground......................... 22
Do You Know Where You're Coming From?... 22
Emergency on Planet Earth (song).... 23
Feels Just Like It Should (Jamiroquai song).. 23
Half the Man (Jamiroquai song) 23
High Times (song) 23
Just Another Story............................. 24
Kids (Jamiroquai song) 25
King for a Day (Jamiroquai song)..... 25
Lifeline (Jamiroquai song)................ 25
Light Years (Jamiroquai song).......... 26
List of Jamiroquai songs 26
Little L... 26
Love Foolosophy............................... 26
Manifest Destiny (Jamiroquai song) . 27
Runaway (Jamiroquai song).............. 27
Scam (Jamiroquai song).................... 27
Seven Days in Sunny June 28
Soul Education 28
Space Cowboy (song) 28
Stillness in Time................................ 29
Supersonic (Jamiroquai song)........... 29
Talullah (Shelter mixes).................... 29
Time Won't Wait 30
Too Young to Die (Jamiroquai song).. 30
Virtual Insanity 30
When You Gonna Learn 31
White Knuckle Ride.......................... 33
You Give Me Something (Jamiroquai song).. 33

Introduction

Purchase of this book entitles you to a free trial membership in the publisher's book club at www.booksllc.net. (Time limited offer.) Simply enter the barcode number from the back cover onto the membership form. The book club entitles you to select from hundreds of thousands of books at no additional charge. You can also download a digital copy of this and related books to read on the go. Simply enter the title or subject onto the search form to find them.

Each chapter in this book ends with a URL to a hyperlinked online version. Type the URL exactly as it appears. If you change the URL's capitalization it won't work. Use the online version to access related pages, websites, footnotes, tables, color photos, updates. Click the version history tab to see the chapter's contributors. Click the edit link to suggest changes.

A large and diverse editor base collaboratively wrote the book, not a single author. After a long process of discussion and debate, the chapters gradually took on a neutral point of view reached through consensus. Additional editors expanded and contributed to chapters striving to achieve balance and comprehensive coverage. This reduced the regional or cultural bias found in many other books and provided access and breadth on subject matter otherwise little documented.

Jamiroquai

Jamiroquai (/dʒəˈmɪrəkwaɪ/) is a British jazz funk and acid jazz band formed in 1992. Jamiroquai were initially the most prominent component in the early-1990s London-based acid jazz movement, alongside groups such as Incognito, the James Taylor Quartet, the Brand New Heavies, Galliano, and Corduroy. Subsequent albums have explored other musical directions such as pop, rock and electronica. Jamiroquai have sold more than 25 million albums worldwide and won a Grammy Award in 1997.

History

Formation

The band name is a portmanteau of Jam session and "iroquai", based on the Iroquois, a Native American tribe. The original band was Jay Kay (vocals), Toby Smith (keyboard), Stuart Zender (bass), Nick Van Gelder (drums), Wallis Buchanan (didgeridoo) and Alec Moran (pipeau). These are the founding members of Jamiroquai and were involved in the writing and production of the first album. The lineup of the band has changed several times, and the longest serving and now core members of the band are lead singer and songwriter Jason "Jay" Kay and drummer Derrick McKenzie (1994). Kay was the impetus behind the formation of Jamiroquai, deciding to form the band after an unsuccessful audition to become the singer of the Brand New Heavies. Despite his self-professed attempts to treat Jamiroquai as a band, Kay has always been at the forefront of how the group is marketed, and has therefore always had the lion's share of media attention, to the point where he is viewed as almost a solo artist.

Sony Music

Jamiroquai's first single, "When You Gonna Learn", was released in 1992 on the Acid Jazz label. Following its success, Kay signed an eight-album record deal with Sony BMG Music Entertainment. The first Sony album, *Emergency on Planet Earth* was released in 1993. It was followed in 1994 by *The Return of the Space Cowboy*. The single "Space Cowboy" gained notice on the charts and in club rotation.

While Jamiroquai was growing in popularity in the UK, Western Europe, Australia, New Zealand and Japan, they remained relatively unknown to U.S and other international audiences. The band's international breakthrough came with the third album, *Travelling Without Moving* in 1996, which yielded two big hits, "Virtual Insanity" and "Cosmic Girl". The success of "Virtual Insanity" was due in part to its Jonathan Glazer-directed video, which featured Kay's dance moves and some physics-defying images. At the 1997 MTV Video Music Awards, the creative music video for "Virtual Insanity" won four awards Best Video, Best Special Effects, Best Cinematography, and Breakthrough Video.

In 2003 Jamiroquai compiled and mixed a DJ mix album for the Late Night Tales series for Azuli Records. The track selection shows some of the band's funk, soul and disco influences, including tracks from The Pointer Sisters, The Commodores, Johnny "Hammond" Smith and Johnny "Guitar" Watson.

The acid jazz flavours and ethnic influences of the first three albums continued with the release of *Synkronized* in 1999. Jay Kay's interest in funk and disco music were shifting the band's directions towards such. By their fifth album, *A Funk Odyssey* (2001), they had evolved so drastically, that some critics and listeners would remark they lost the 'Jamiroquai sound'. With the departure of more and more original band members, including Wallis Buchanan and his didgeridoo, Jamiroquai had become a very different band than that of 1992. In spite of the changes, the fifth album's first single, "Little L", reached #1 in many charts worldwide.

Their sixth album, titled *Dynamite* was released on 20 June 2005. It reached #3 on the UK charts. The first single, "Feels Just Like It Should" was released early in June, the second, "Seven Days in Sunny June" released on 15 August 2005, followed by the third, "(Don't) Give Hate A Chance" on 7 November 2005.

Jamiroquai released a greatest hits collection, *High Times: Singles 1992-2006* in November 2006. The release of this album marked the end of Kay's eight-album contract with Sony. The album reached the number 1 spot in the UK album chart after its first week of release. The album featured two new tracks, "Runaway" and "Radio". On 18 September 2006, "Runaway" was given its first play by UK radio stations. It was released as a single on 30 October 2006. Kay remarked that compilation was released purely out of contractual obligation: "2006, they're out of the picture."

Jamiroquai have had 13 nominations for The Brit Awards, and have yet to win one.

In October 2006, Jamiroquai recorded a live session for *Live from Abbey Road* at Abbey Road Studios. Their performance was shown alongside those of Damien Rice and the Goo Goo Dolls on the UK's Channel 4 in January 2007. In May 2006 Jamiroquai performed during the Laureus Sports Awards in Barcelona; the event was later televised by NBC in June.

In March 2006, Jamiroquai announced their switch to Columbia Records. Future releases will appear under the Columbia imprint.

During February in 2007 Jamiroquai performed the record breaking Gig in the Sky in association with Sony Ericsson.

After leaving Sony, the band began to work on their seventh project, and several collaborations and side-projects. In a very short mid-2007 interview with Jamirotalk, drummer Derick McKenzie expressed his satisfaction with leaving Sony as the beginning of a period in which the band will have more creative control over their own work, together with plenty of room for experimentation and lack of pressure from a record company.

Rock Dust Light Star and beyond

On 11 January 2008, Jay Kay himself posted a news item in which he thanked everyone who wished him the best for his birthday, and announced that the writing process for the new album had just begun. Only a day earlier, drummer Derick McKenzie posted an article on his MySpace weblog that the recording process for the same record had also begun.

On 15 January 2008, the band confirmed that the recording process had begun. According to the news item, eleven tracks had already been written for the new album, with more to come. As of 25 July 2010, the only known track name for the 7th album is "Rock Dust Light Star" which has been performed live and confirmed by Kay himself to be on the new album. On 13 February 2008, the band announced from their website that it would perform at the *World Stage of the Rock in Rio — Madrid festival*, being held in Arganda del Rey, Madrid with others artists who have (then) yet to be announced.

On 28 February 2008, Jamiroquai performed at the Khodynka Arena in Moscow, Russia at the launch of the new Audi A4 car. On 22 June 2008, Jamiroquai performed at the Wianki Festival in Kraków, Poland. On 4 July 2008, the band performed in front of a 75,000-people audience in the Rock in Rio Madrid festival. On 5 April 2009, Jamiroquai performed at the closing concert of Malaysian F1 Grand Prix in Sepang International Circuit Malaysia, and on the 9 April Jamiroquai played at the Sentul International Convention Centre in Jakarta, Indonesia.

On 24 August 2009, Derrick McKenzie was interviewed on playvybz.com and talked about the upcoming album. He stated that Jamiroquai was then signed with Universal Records (UK) and that they had recorded more than 40 new tracks. Also the new album will be recorded live and have a style similar to the first three albums with the use of strings and horns. He claims the album will have less of a "disco sound" and will be a lot more funky and soulful. The album is uninfluenced by major record labels and will bring forth a new direction for the band.

During the first week of February 2010, Jay Kay mentioned the upcoming album on Jamiroquai's Facebook site, saying, "Hi Everybody, just wanted to say how amazing it is to have so many Friends on Facebook, half a million I believe. Therefore it feels like the right time to let you know that we are alive and kicking and in the final stages of our 8th album. I really can't wait to get out there and play it for you live in the very near future. Sending you all lots of good luck and love, Jay."

The first week of April 2010, Jay Kay announced on the Jamiroquai Facebook page that Jamiroquai would be supporting Stevie Wonder. "I am thrilled and excited to be supporting such a luminary as Stevie Wonder, can't wait to see you all there and get to play some stuff from the new album. Love Jay".

Jay Kay has mentioned on an Italian website, CNRmedia.com, that the new album, still untitled, will tentatively be released in September 2010.

Based on official mailing list e-mails (related to jamiroquai.com and Jamiroquai's record label) promoting a contest, Jamiroquai are now signed to Mercury Records/Universal On 24 June 2010, the band played a warm-up gig at Debut London to a small crowd. The set list featured songs from all the Jamiroquai albums except for Dynamite as well as a brand new song titled "*Rock Dust Light Star*". On 26 June upon supporting Stevie Wonder at Hard Rock Calling Festival at Hyde Park, a new album was confirmed and stated to be released in October 2010, and the photography for it was taken in which Jay Kay posed in costume in front of the crowd behind him. On July 21 at a concert in Nîmes, Jay told the crowd their new album would be out in November and Paul Turner also told Funky Tivi (a French web TV) music style of the new album will be rather funk/rock. (source : http://funkytivi.jimdo.com/).

On 16 August 2010 it was announced on Jamiroquai.com that the new album will be titled *Rock Dust Light Star* and be released in November 2010.

On 1 September 2010, Jay Kay featured on The Chris Moyles Show (This edition hosted by Vernon Kay) and the Single White Knuckle Ride was played for the first time, live on air. It was met with massive critical praise from people texting the show, many of them claiming that "Funk is back".

On 1 October 2010, Jamiroquai appeared on UK television's Later...with Jools Holland. *Rock Dust Light Star* was the first performance of the show, and was well received. They also performed *Deeper Underground* and *Blue Skies*.

On November 1, 2010, they released their long anticipated seventh album, Rock Dust Light Star. Recorded in Jay Kay's home studio in Buckinghamshire, it saw a return to their earlier, less pop-like sound. Despite both singles, Blue Skies and White Knuckle Ride reaching into Top 100 charts worldwide, the album sold a mere 34,378 copies on its debut, around half the amount sold of the previous album Dynamite.

Buffalo Man

Buffalo Man is the name of the silhouette character featured on most of the covers of Jamiroquai's releases. It was created by Jay Kay between 1992 and 1993.

The original Buffalo Man slightly modified since 1997.

Origins

Buffalo Man was created sometime prior to the release of their 1992 single *When You Gonna Learn*, allegedly it was originally sketched by the band's primary songwriter and front-man Jason Kay as *Buffalo Man* is seemingly a self portrait silhouette of Jason wearing a buffalo hat. The mark has been used on almost every commercial (and sometimes non-commercial) release of the band's output in some form or another; usually the unique symbol is pictured unaltered, but there have been times where it is shown in a stylised manner to suit the artwork or song.

The animated Buffalo Man as he appears in the (Don't) Give Hate a Chance music video.

Notable variations

Over the years, Buffalo Man has seen some temporary changes or interesting thematic uses:

"Half the Man", *The Return of the Space Cowboy* For the single "Half The Man", *Buffalo Man* is on the cover as a keyring with a heart in the clasp representing the fact it is a love song and the keyring itself is split down the middle in two halves to represent the song title. *Buffalo Man* also has a silver heart.

"Space Cowboy", *The Return of the Space Cowboy* For the single "Space Cowboy", *Buffalo Man* is present on the cover as a shaped cigarette paper for a half-complete cannabis joint, in reference to the song's praise of the drug.

"Virtual Insanity", *Travelling Without Moving* For the single of "Virtual Insanity", Buffalo Man appears in the place of the Ferrari horse in an homage to Jason's love of sports cars. For the album cover to *Travelling Without Moving*, the artwork is similar, but takes on an embossed effect and is seen on a metal grille.

"Cosmic Girl", "Everyday" For these two releases, Buffalo Man is pictured with a star over his heart and two intersecting orbital rings.

Synkronized While the design remained fundamentally unaltered, Buffalo Man has been turned into a laser-cut mirror and photographed from interesting angles by Midori Tsukagoshi. On some editions, for the disc itself, no ink has been used on the character, but the same stone background found on the front cover has been used for the rest of the disc, thus allowing the consumer to recreate the photographed effect.

A Funk Odyssey For this album, the Buffalo Man was notably absent from the cover; instead, the laser lights formed an outline of the Buffalo Man logo, which could be seen much more clearly in the album's liner notes.

Dynamite The US release and the double-disc Australian Tour Edition featured a gold Buffalo Man. Other releases saw a picture of Jay Kay instead.

Rock Dust Light Star The letter "i" in the title is replaced with the Buffalo Man, making the first appearance in a Jamiroquai album cover since 1999's *Synkronized* (not counting the alternative artwork for *Dynamite*).

Text logo

Jamiroquai

The regular text logo.

Just like the Buffalo Man, the Jamiroquai text logo has also had several variations depending on the theme. The oldest version of the logo is the one seen on the Acid Jazz Records release of When You Gonna Learn. In comparison to the current text logo one can see that the old Acid Jazz Records version of the logo was more angular at points, together with the letters being much thinner. Several variations of the current logo also exist. Releases of "Cosmic Girl" and the promo CD of "Everyday" had replaced the dots above the 'i' letters with stars. Other slight, temporary variations include a slight vertical stretch of the typeface, as seen on the cover art of *A Funk Odyssey* and *Rock Dust Light Star*.

Source (edited): "http://en.wikipedia.org/wiki/Jamiroquai"

Jamiroquai concerts

In Fall 2010 Jamiroquai embarked on a world tour to promote their latest studio album Rock Dust Light Star (released on November 1, 2010).

European Tour 2011

- 18/03/2011 Zurich (Hallenstadion) Germany
- 21/03/2011 Hamburg (O2 World) Germany
- 23/03/2011 Paris (POPB) France
- ~~24/03/2011 Lyon (Halle Tony Garnier) France~~ {CANCELLED}
- 26/03/2011 Munich (Olympiahalle) Germany
- 28/03/2011 Vienna (Stadthalle) Austria
- 30/03/2011 Assago (near Milan) (Mediolanum Forum) Italy
- 31/03/2011 Mantova (Pala Bam) Italy
- 02/04/2011 Turin (Pala Olympico) Italy
- 03/04/2011 Florence (Mandela Forum) Italy
- 05/04/2011 Luxemburg (Roc Hall) Luxembourg
- 06/04/2011 Stuttgart (Porsche Arena) Germany
- 08/04/2011 Berlin (O2 World) Germany
- 10/04/2011 Brussels (Forest National) Belgium
- 12/04/2011 Oberhausen (Arena) Germany
- 13/04/2011 Rotterdam (Ahoy) The Netherlands
- 15/04/2011 London (O2 Arena) UK
- 17/04/2011 Birmingham (LG Arena) UK
- 19/04/2011 Manchester (MEN Arena) UK
- 20/04/2011 Glasgow (SE&CC) UK
- 21/04/2011 Zagreb (INmusic Festival) {not certain}
- 29/04/2011 Santiago (Colors Festival - Movistar Arena) Chile

- 08/06/2011 Tallinn (Saku Suurhall Arena) Estonia
- 18/06/2011 Warsaw (Orange Festival) Poland
- 21/06/2011 Zagreb (INmusic Festival) Croatia
- 24/06/2011 Razlog (Elevation Festival) Bulgaria {not certain}
- 09/07/2011 Novi Sad (Exit Festival) Serbia
- 13/07/2011 Straubing (Jazz Donau) Germany
- 14/07/2011 Mainz (Zollhafen Nordmole) Germany
- 16/07/2011 Bern (Gurten Festival) Switzerland
- 17/07/2011 Ulm (Radio Festival) Germany
- 21/07/2011 Padova (Piazzola Sul Brenta) Italy
- 22/07/2011 Rome (Ippodromo Delle Capannelle) Italy
- 24/07/2011 Lucca (Piazza Napoleone) Italy
- 28/07/2011 Vienne (near Lyon) (Théâtre Antique) France

Source (edited): "http://en.wikipedia.org/wiki/Jamiroquai_concerts"

Jamiroquai discography

The discography of Jamiroquai, a British jazz funk and acid jazz band.

Compilation albums
- *Jay's Selection* (1996, released exclusively in Japan)
- *In Store Jam* (promo, 1997)
- *Late Night Tales: Jamiroquai* (10 November 2003)
- *High Times: Singles 1992–2006* (6 November 2006) - #1 UK, #5 ITA, #4 JPN UK: 2x Platinum

Live albums
- *JAZZiroquai* (1998)

Remix albums
- *1999 Remixes* (1999)

Video albums
- *Corner of the Earth* (8 July 2002) - #31 UK
- *Live in Verona* (11 November 2002) - #7 UK
- *High Times: Singles 1992-2006* (6 November 2006)
- *Jamiroquai – Live at Montreux 2003* (22 October 2007)

Source (edited): "http://en.wikipedia.org/wiki/Jamiroquai_discography"

Jay Kay

Jason "Jay Kay" Cheetham (born on 30 December 1969 in Stretford, Manchester, England), is a Grammy Award-winning English artist, best known as the lead singer of the acid jazz band Jamiroquai.

Career

Kay formed Jamiroquai with members Toby Smith (keyboards), Stuart Zender (bass), Nick Van Gelder (drums), Wallis Buchanan (didgeridoo) and Alec Moran (pipeau) together with guest appearances by Gavin Dodds (guitar), Maurizio Ravelico (percussion) and Johnny Thirkell (horns) amongst others, both on the band's debut album and on their first tour.

Jamiroquai has sold over thirty million albums, and has spent a collective 162 weeks on the UK singles chart between 1992 and 2006 with Kay's personal wealth said to be around £40 million. He appeared on the *Sunday Times Rich List 2004* at joint-950th. The *Sunday Times Rich List 2008* has him tied for #1,794, with £40 million.

After the huge success of Jamiroquai's first single, *When You Gonna Learn*, a $1.9 million, eight album deal was signed with Sony Music Entertainment. The band's first album was *Emergency on Planet Earth*. The relationship with Sony ended in 2007.

The band's third album, *Travelling Without Moving*, generated international attention with the ground breaking video of *Virtual Insanity* which earned Jamiroquai four MTV Video Music Awards. Since then, their fourth album, *Synkronized*, has done just as well; it was recorded in Kay's home studio located in the garden of his 500-year-old, 11-bedroom Buckinghamshire mansion.

Kay has previously stated that he would like his band to continue writing music for another 15–20 years. However it was reported in February 2007 that Kay had wanted to quit music. This was denied on Jamiroquai's official website the day after.

Headgear

Kay wearing a headdress during a concert

Kay is well known for his array of elaborate hats and headgear. When appearing professionally (in concerts, interviews etc.) he has been referred to as "cat in the hat" for his love of headgear. It is said that he has over 50 different hats that he wears at concerts and in public. He has stated publicly that some of them were made by his own mother.

Kay's most recognizable headgear is his mirrored "feather headdress" seen on the cover of *High Times: Singles*

1992–2006.

TV performances

Some of Kay's more notable British television appearances include co-starring in an episode of the BBC series *The Naked Chef* alongside chef Jamie Oliver. He has also performed on the series *Strictly Come Dancing* singing Canned Heat. As a keen sports car driver he is also known for his appearances on *Top Gear* and for a time held the record for the fastest celebrity lap in the Chevrolet Lacetti from more than 50 other celebrity drivers.

The day before Jamiroquai performed their new single, White Knuckle Ride, on *The X Factor* on 31 October 2010, Kay was quoted by *The Sun* as saying of the show's judges Cheryl Cole and Dannii Minogue: "What are they going to tell me about fucking music? ... When have you ever done anything? You're useless. The pair of you. I mean you look great and I'd like to fucking shag you but that's all." During his performance on the show, the pair talked continuously and refused to applaud at the end. Notably, neither of the other two judges stood up either.

Paparazzi confrontations

In 2001, Kay was charged with assaulting a photographer and damaging his camera outside a nightclub. Kay pleaded not guilty and the charges were later dropped. On 12 September 2006, Kay was cautioned by police over an incident outside a London nightclub. He allegedly assaulted two photographers.

Personal life

Kay's father is Portuguese. Kay's mother is former singer and television personality Karen Kay. His primary home is in Buckinghamshire, but also he owns homes in Westminster and Gairloch.

In a 2010 interview, Kay indicated that at one time he had a "substantial" cocaine habit. He has however been free of drugs since 2003.

Kay continues to support the Burma Campaign UK and the need for democracy in Burma. He is also a patron of the Captive Animals Protection Society, a charity campaigning for an end to the use of animals in circuses, zoos and exotic pet trade. He has spoken out against animal exploitation for entertainment.

Cars and vehicles

Kay has a strong interest in exotic cars and owns over 30 luxury cars, mainly sports cars. His love of motors was expressed with the release of the album *Travelling Without Moving*. The album's cover featured an adaptation of the "Buffalo Man" logo and the Ferrari crest. Three of his cars appeared in the video for the song *Cosmic Girl*. In total he has 37 vehicles including what he calls "staff cars".

He owns Ferraris, including an Enzo. A combination of cars and music is evident in the song *Black Devil Car* on the album *Dynamite* which is a tribute to his black Ferrari Enzo. The Enzo suffered damage to the windows after an altercation with hotel chef Aaron Billington at the Brudenell Hotel in Aldeburgh, Suffolk.

Kay's love of fast cars has occasionally landed him in legal trouble. In May 1998, Kay was caught driving at 111 mph and his licence was suspended for 42 days. He said in an interview: "I should count myself lucky. I've clocked up 175 mph on a public road. If I'd been caught doing that, it would have been a prison sentence." He appeared in court in Scotland to face charges for speeding after being clocked at 105 mph in a Mercedes-Benz G-Class, on 26 February 2004. The speed limit for the road was 70 mph. He was later banned from driving for six months.

Kay participated in the 2007 Gumball 3000 rally as part of Team Addidas in a brand new Maserati Quattroporte. In 2010 he took part in the Mille Miglia in his Maserati A6G/54.

He holds the record on the BBC show *Top Gear* for the fastest lap in the (now retired) Chevrolet Lacetti on the "Star in a Reasonably-Priced Car" segment. His time of 1:45.81 was four-hundredths of a second ahead of Kevin McCloud, one-tenth of a second ahead of Brian Johnson, lead singer of the rock band AC/DC, and one tenth of a second above then-leader, Simon Cowell. He was invited back as Cowell had been "on the top for long enough".

Kay also likes motorcycles and was at the Ace Cafe to see Charley Boorman off for his television series *By Any Means*. He rides a Rizla Suzuki GSXR-600. He owns a motorhome, and holds a C LGV (class 2) driving license just to drive it. He persuaded his close friend James Martin to also purchase one. Kay also leases a Robinson R44 helicopter, registration G-JKAY.

Source (edited): "http://en.wikipedia.org/wiki/Jay_Kay"

Space Clav

"**Space Clav**" is the B-side to the "Half the Man" single. The song is a live performance from the band Jamiroquai, which was first featured in their live performance at Kanagawa, Japan in 1993.

The original live track has a duration of 5:31 and features the popular members such as Stuart Zender, Toby Smith, DJ-DZIRE and also Nick van Geldar. Jason Kay apparently wrote the song along with a few of the members but this has not been officially confirmed.

Source (edited): "http://en.wikipedia.org/wiki/Space_Clav"

1999 Remixes

1999 Remixes is the third compilation album released by British acid jazz band Jamiroquai. Released on September 20, 1999, the album features a selection of remixes based on tracks included on the group's fourth studio album, *Synkronized*. The album was initially available as a package of four 12" records, before being made available on Limited Edition CD and Cassette formats in early 2000.

Source (edited): "http://en.wikipedia.org/wiki/1999_Remixes"

A Funk Odyssey

A Funk Odyssey is the fifth studio album by British acid jazz band Jamiroquai, released on 3 September 2001 in the United Kingdom, and 11 September 2001 in the United States. A promotional accompaniment to the album, entitled *An Online Odyssey*, was made available to members of the group's official website in Summer 2001.

Background

Combining features of disco, funk and electronica, the release of the album represented the peak of international commercial success for Jamiroquai, and in the ensuing world tour the group became a household name in many countries. The sleeve art of *A Funk Odyssey* features Jay Kay posed in front of a series of lasers that form the famous "Buffalo Man" logo, making it the first Jamiroquai album not to feature the logo prominently on its cover. The album marks a departure from the band's previous acid jazz sound; the band finds themselves in a disco/funk vibe, and is also very focused on an electronica sound, evident especially in "Twenty Zero One" and "Stop Don't Panic". A popular fan interpretation is that "Main Vein" is a song written about Denise van Outen, Jay's ex-girlfriend, but from her perspective; the song would have thus featured a female vocalist and would showcase the same fight shown in "Little L" but from Denise's perspective. A test pressing of the album features an instrumental of "Main Vein", which supports this theory.

Reception

Initial critical response to *A Funk Odyssey* was generally mixed. At Metacritic, which assigns a normalized rating out of 100 to reviews from mainstream critics, the album has received an average score of 58, based on 13 reviews. *Q* magazine (September 2001, p. 112) - 4 stars out of 5 - "A certified thoroughbred. This time, there's a bankable chorus or barbed sentiment for every mirror-ball moment....demonstrating that no-one does sci-fi boogie quite as well as he does sci-fi boogie." *CMJ* (17 September 2001, p. 12) - "Works as the perfect mixed tape to snap your fingers to on your way to another universe."

Tracklisting

- "Feel So Good" – 5:21 (Kay/Smith)
- "Little L" – 4:55 (Kay/Smith)
- "You Give Me Something" – 3:23 (Kay/Harris/Fyffe)
- "Corner of the Earth" – 5:40 (Kay/Harris)
- "Love Foolosophy" – 3:45 (Kay/Smith)
- "Stop Don't Panic" – 4:34 (Kay/Harris/Fyffe)
- "Black Crow" – 4:02 (Kay/Harris/Fyffe)
- "Main Vein" – 5:05 (Kay)
- "Twenty Zero One" – 5:15 (Kay)
- "Picture Of My Life" - 4:11 (Kay/Harris/Smith)
- "So Good To Feel Real" (Hidden Track) – 2:14

Special Edition Bonus Disc

- "Space Cowboy" (Classic Club Mix)
- "Supersonic" (Dirty Rotten Scoundrels Vocal)
- "Deeper Underground"
- "Little L" (Bob Sinclair Remix)
- "You Give Me Something" (Full Intention Remix)
- "Main Vein" (Live)

Original Test Pressing

- "Feel So Good" (Uncut) – 6:24
- "Little L" (Extra Percussion) – 4:55
- "You Give Me Something" (Uncut) – 5:16
- "Interlude #1" – 0:35
- "Main Vein" (No Vocals - Cut) – 4:51
- "Corner Of The Earth" (Vocal Variation) – 5:40
- "Twenty Zero One" (Uncut) – 8:29
- "Black Crow" (Vocal Variation) – 4:02
- "Interlude #2" – 1:22
- "Do It Like We Used To Do" (Edited) – 6:49
- "Stop Don't Panic" (Uncut) – 5:31
- "Interlude #3" – 0:20
- "Picture Of My Life" (Vocal Variation - Cut) – 3:46
- "So Good To Feel Real" – 2:14

Outtakes

- "Cannabliss" - A track which, after being scrapped from the project, featured as the introduction to "Corner of the Earth". Jay claimed the track "wasn't even half complete" at the time of going to press.
- "A Funk Odyssey" - Performed by the group while on tour. It is unknown whether this track is an outtake from the album, a live-only track, or both.
- "Shoot The Moon" - A further outtake from the album. The track was performed live at least twice, once at the Montreux Jazz Festival in 2003, and once at a concert in Turkey. A widely-circulated recording of the song being played at the festival exists, and can be found on the group's official website for download. One interesting fact about the song is that it was intended to

have a horn section. The band did not have a horn section at the time, so the electric guitar had to substitute the horns. A studio version was never recorded.
- "Interludes #1, #2 & #3" - The test pressing of the album featured three interludes. The first features band frontman Jay in an electronically manipulated monologue, asking himself why he would want to "shut down the funk assembly unit." The second interlude is a beatbox track, which was later sampled in the single "Feels Just Like It Should", while the third features Strauss' "The Blue Danube" being faded in slowly at a low volume. A case of synchronicity occurs when the test pressing is played to Stanley Kubrick's film adaptation of Arthur C. Clarke's *2001: A Space Odyssey*.

Source (edited): "http://en.wikipedia.org/wiki/A_Funk_Odyssey"

Dynamite (Jamiroquai album)

Dynamite is Jamiroquai's sixth studio album, released in June 2005. Produced by Mike Spencer and Jay Kay, it is perhaps their most diverse work to date, featuring electronic, funk, disco, house and acoustic tracks.

Album information

Dynamite was released on 20th September, 2005. The album was released after the 2004 hit movie Napoleon Dynamite featured the Jamiroquai song Canned Heat in its climactic dance scene. The second single, "Seven Days in Sunny June", was released in the UK in August 2005, peaking at #14 on the UK singles chart. The song also featured in the film "The Devil Wears Prada" (2006). On 7 November, 2005, "(Don't) Give Hate A Chance" was released as the third single from the album. The politically-driven video for the track, which can be seen in its entirety at the band's website, is Jamiroquai's first animated clip; it features a Buffalo Man, complete with buffalo-horned hat, sunglasses, and tracksuit. The clip helped the track score Top 20 showings in UK charts such as the Smash Hits and hit40uk charts (both of which take in radio and video airplay, not just sales). However, the track bowed meekly at No.27 on the official UK singles chart. The album was recorded in many locations, including Jay's personal Chillington Studios, and Los Angeles.

Reception

The album bowed at No.3 in the United Kingdom, becoming the first Jamiroquai album to chart outside the top two spots. However, with other solid new albums from Coldplay, Foo Fighters and others in the top five, it was still a strong success for Jamiroquai.

"Feels Just Like It Should" was the first single release, reaching No.8 in its first week on the UK charts. It has since become a No.1 hit on the *Billboard* dance charts in the United States. The album was also certified Gold in Japan for selling 100,000 copies.

Uncut (p.102) - 3 stars out of 5 - "Jay Kay returns with another blast of super-slick soul..."

Vibe (p.150) - "[T]he space cowboys return with a vengeance, sounding funky as ever."

Track listing

CD Release
- "Feels Just Like It Should" (Kay) – 4:34
- "Dynamite" (Johnson, Kay) – 4:57
- "Seven Days in Sunny June" (Johnson, Kay) – 3:59
- "Electric Mistress" (Harris, Johnson, Kay) – 3:56
- "Starchild" (Harris, Johnson, Kay) – 5:13
- "Love Blind" (Harris, Johnson, Kay) – 3:35
- "Talullah" (Harris, Kay) – 6:04
- "(Don't) Give Hate a Chance" (Harris, Johnson, Kay) – 5:02
- "World That He Wants" (Johnson, Kay) – 3:14
- "Black Devil Car" (Harris, Kay) – 4:45
- "Hot Tequila Brown" (Harris, Johnson, Kay) – 4:40
- "Time Won't Wait" (Harris, Johnson, Kay) – 5:01

DualDisc release
- Entire album in Enhanced Stereo – 54:59
- "Feels Just Like It Should" (Video) – 4:34
- "Seven Days in Sunny June" (Video) – 3:59
- "Feels Just Like It Should" (The Making Of) – 10:00
- Additional album art

Australian Tour Edition Bonus Remix CD
- "Don't Give Hate a Chance" (Steve Mac Classic Remix)
- "Don't Give Hate a Chance" (Freemasons Remix)
- "Don't Give Hate a Chance" (Freemasons Dub)
- "Seven Days in Sunny June" (Ashley Beedle Heavy Disco Dub)
- "Seven Days in Sunny June" (Kraak & Smaak Remix)
- "Seven Days in Sunny June" (Blackbeard Remix)
- "Feels Just Like It Should" (Mark Ronson Remix)
- "Feels Just Like It Should" (Timo Maas Remix)

Personnel
- Sola Akingbola – percussion
- Pablo Arraya – engineer
- Richard Bignell – engineer
- Bridgette Bryant Blades – backing vocals
- Alexandra Brown – backing vocals
- Luke Cohen – studio assistant
- Tom Coyne – mastering
- Reginald Dozier – engineer
- Valerie Etienne – backing vocals
- Hazel Fernandez – backing vocals
- Nick Ferrero – engineer
- Nathan Haines – flute, saxophone
- Rob Harris – guitar
- Randy Hope-Taylor – bass
- Matt Johnson – piano, keyboards, fender rhodes, synthesizer bass
- Vann Johnson – backing vocals
- Charlie Lightening – photography

- Miaer "DJ Snare" Lloyd – scratching
- Audrey Martells – backing vocals
- Derrick McIntyre – bass
- Derrick McKenzie – drums, hi hat
- Alex Meadows – bass
- Ricky Pope – engineer
- Samantha Smith – backing vocals
- Mike Spencer – programming, producer, engineer, mixing
- Benjamin Wright – strings, string arrangements

Source (edited): "http://en.wikipedia.org/wiki/Dynamite_(Jamiroquai_album)"

Emergency on Planet Earth

Emergency on Planet Earth is the debut album of the band Jamiroquai. Released in 1993, the album features strong elements of the mixture of the R&B, and funk genres, but it is notable for being one of the definitive acid-jazz albums. The recurring theme on the album deals with lyrics about world issues and self-consciousness, along with several jazz instrumentals that made the album a success in the band's native country, the UK.

Album information

The album produced several well-received singles, including "Too Young To Die" and "Blow Your Mind".

In the game *Secret Files: Tunguska*, a CD case of this album can be spotted on a desk in an office.

The album was listed in the music reference book *1001 Albums You Must Hear Before You Die*.

Reception

- *Entertainment Weekly* (13 August 1993, p. 74) - "...turn out gritty organic grooves with enthusiasm..." Rating: B+
- *Q* (March 2001, p. 124) - 4 stars out of 5 - "A funky and beautiful record, a contender for best British soul album of the '90s, and frankly better than anything Stevie Wonder has made since Hotter Than July."
- *BBC Music* (12 December 2008)) - "...the album was an infectious, funk mezze of trumpets, saxophones, didgeridoos and flutes, spawning the hit singles Too Young To Die and Blow Your Mind which both entered the UK Top 10 in 1993."

CD Release
LP Release
- "When You Gonna Learn" (Extended J.K. Mix) – 6:21
- "Too Young to Die" (Extended J.K Mix) – 10:12
- "Hooked Up" – 4:35
- "If I Like It, I Do It" (Extended Mix) – 6:54
- "Music of the Mind" – 6:22
- "Emergency on Planet Earth" (Extended Mix) – 4:13
- "Whatever It Is, I Just Can't Stop" – 4:07
- "Blow Your Mind" – 8:32
- "Revolution 1993" – 10:16
- "Didgin' Out" – 2:37

Singles
- "When You Gonna Learn?" - October 19, 1992
- "Too Young to Die" - March 1, 1993
- "Blow Your Mind" - May 24, 1993
- "Emergency on Planet Earth" - August 2, 1993

Personnel
- Jason Kay – vocals
- Wallis Buchanan – didjeridoo
- Toby Smith – keyboards, string arrangements
- Stuart Zender – bass
- Nick Van Gelder – drums
- Gary Barnacle – flute, saxophone, brass Arrangement
- Simon Bartholomew – guitar
- Glen Nightingale – guitar
- DJ Dzire – turntables
- Kofi Kari Kari – percussion
- Maurizio Ravalio – percussion
- Richard Edwards – trombone
- John Thirkell – trumpet, flugelhorn
- Gavin Dodds – guitar (on track 1)
- Mike Smith – saxophone, flute (on track 1)
- Linda Lewis – background vocals (on track 2)
- Vanessa Simon – background vocals (on track 9)
- The Reggae Philharmonic Strings – strings

Source (edited): "http://en.wikipedia.org/wiki/Emergency_on_Planet_Earth"

High Times: Singles 1992–2006

High Times: Singles 1992–2006 is a collection of Jamiroquai's hits, and includes two new songs: "Runaway" and "Radio." Most of the band's best known songs are included, with two notable exceptions: "King for a Day" and "You Give Me Something", although a remix of the latter appears on CD 2 of the Special Edition release. Several other singles were also left out: "Stillness in Time", "Half the Man", "Light Years", "Kids", "Black Capricorn Day", and "Supersonic", although some of these were featured on international editions. The album ended Jamiroquai's contract with Sony BMG.

Upon release, the album reached the top of the BBC Radio 1 albums chart. number 5 in Italy and number 1 in Japan. It reached the top of the UK Album Chart. Most of the tracks on the compilation album are "radio" or "single edits". The sleeve art for *High Times* features Jason Kay's signature Silver Crown headpiece photographed on a beach with rock formations. There are multiple versions of the release, including but not limited to a "regular" edition; a "Deluxe" edition, which includes a disc of remixes; a Japan-only CD/DVD release; and a UK DVD of music videos. The album has been certified platinum for physical sales in Japan.

Promotion

High Times: Singles received relatively heavy promotion for a "Greatest hits" album. Posters promoting the album were found in some cities, and very many promotional performances were also held, most notable one being the London Jazz Cafe performance, which is notable for being the first Jamiroquai performance in the last few years that included wind instruments. The album was also heavily promoted via the internet, most notably via Yahoo! Answers, and a competition to win an MP3 player that contains the new album.

In promotional images, a reflection of the photographer shooting the image can be seen in the hat's surface, although in the cover of the actual release the reflection has been erased from the image.

Track listing

Disc 1

- "When You Gonna Learn" – 3:49
- "Too Young to Die" – 3:23
- "Blow Your Mind" – 3:56
- "Emergency on Planet Earth" – 3:37
- "Space Cowboy" – 3:37
- "Virtual Insanity" – 3:49
- "Cosmic Girl" – 3:47
- "Alright" – 3:42
- "High Times" – 4:10
- "Deeper Underground" – 4:46
- "Canned Heat" – 3:48
- "Little L" – 3:59
- "Love Foolosophy" – 3:47
- "Corner of the Earth" – 3:56
- "Feels Just Like It Should" – 4:33
- "Seven Days in Sunny June" – 4:02
- "(Don't) Give Hate a Chance" – 3:51
- "Runaway" – 3:46
- "Radio" – 4:12
- "Half the Man" – 4:50 (Japanese bonus track)

Disc 2

- "Runaway" (Tom Belton Remix) - 3:29 (Japanese bonus track)
- "Feels So Good" (Knee Deep Remix) - 3:44 (Japanese bonus track)
- "Emergency on Planet Earth" (Masters at Work remix) – 7:10
- "Space Cowboy" (David Morales remix) – 7:52
- "Love Foolosophy" (Knee Deep mix) – 8:27 (Not included on the japanese press)
- "Little L" (Bob Sinclar mix) – 7:24
- "Cosmic Girl" (Tom Belton mix) – 7:46
- "Dynamite" (Phil Asher remix) – 7:40
- "Seven Days in Sunny June" (Ashley Beedle remix) – 7:54
- "Virtual Insanity" (Salaam Remi remix) – 5:41
- "You Give Me Something" (Blacksmith R&B mix) – 4:02
- "Supersonic" (Restless Souls/Phil Asher remix) – 8:26
- "Love Foolosophy" (Mondo Grosso Love Acoustic Mix) – 4:43 (Japanese bonus track)

Bonus DVD (Japanese Only Release)

- "Too Young to Die"
- "Emergency on Planet Earth"
- "Space Cowboy"
- "Half the Man"
- "Virtual Insanity"
- "Cosmic Girl"
- "Deeper Underground"
- "Canned Heat"
- "Little L"
- "Love Foolosophy"
- "Feels Just Like It Should"
- "Seven Days in Sunny June"
- "Runaway"

High Times: Singles 1992–2006 DVD

The cover of Jamiroquai's *High Times* DVD

- "When You Gonna Learn"
- "Too Young to Die"
- "Blow Your Mind"
- "Emergency On Planet Earth"
- "If I Like It, I Do It" (Compilation Video)
- "Space Cowboy"
- "Half the Man"
- "Light Years"
- "Stillness in Time"
- "Virtual Insanity"
- "Cosmic Girl"
- "Alright"
- "High Times"
- "Deeper Underground"
- "Canned Heat"
- "Supersonic"
- "King for a Day"
- "Black Capricorn Day" (not actually listed on the package)
- "Little L"
- "You Give Me Something"
- "Love Foolosophy"
- "Corner of the Earth"
- "Feels Just Like It Should"
- "Seven Days in Sunny June"
- "(Don't) Give Hate a Chance"

Bonus Material:

- Making of "Little L"

In Store Jam

In Store Jam is the second compilation album released by British acid jazz band Jamiroquai. Released as a promotional album in 1997, the record features a selection of tracks from all three of the group's early studio albums, as well as an additional live recording of Kool & the Gang's "Hollywood Swinging". All of the tracks from the album have, or been considered to become, singles. The album was only released in the United States. Two versions of the release were available: a standard CD, and a Cassette Tape release, retitled **Sampler**, with the addition of an extra track.

Tracklisting

- "Everyday" - 4:03 (Cassette Tape Only)
- "Virtual Insanity" - 5:43
- "Alright" - 4:25
- "Light Years" - 3:59
- "Space Cowboy" - 6:23
- "Emergency On Planet Earth" - 4:13
- "Too Young To Die" - 6:24
- "Hollywood Swinging" (Live In The Chicago Riviera) - 5:33

Source (edited): "http://en.wikipedia.org/wiki/In_Store_Jam"

Jay's Selection

Jay's Selection is the first compilation album released by British acid jazz band Jamiroquai. The album features a selection of tracks chosen and mixed by lead singer Jay Kay. The album was released exclusively in Japan in 1996,, and has never been available in the United Kingdom. Although Jay's vocals do not appear on any of the tracks, you can clearly hear that the group have added their usual acid jazz theme to each recording.

Tracklisting

- "Footsteps In The Dark"
- "Lady Sun"
- "Sun Goddess"
- "In Time"
- "The World Is Yours"
- "Everybody Is A Star"
- "Free"
- "Fight The Power"
- "I'm Kurious"
- "For The Love Of Money"
- "Chameleon"

Source (edited): "http://en.wikipedia.org/wiki/Jay%27s_Selection"

Late Night Tales: Jamiroquai

Late Night Tales: Jamiroquai is the fourth compilation album released by British acid jazz band Jamiroquai. Released on November 10, 2003, it is the group's second compilation album not to include any songs from the group themselves. The album is the tenth release in the Late Night Tales series. A special edition of the album was released in September 2005, with the addition of a Buffalo Man embossed slipcase.. The album has been re-mastered and re-released in November 2010 and is available on iTunes.

Tracklisting

- Pointer Sisters - "Happiness" – 3:53
- The Commodores - "Girl I Think The World About You" – 4:26
- Rufus & Chaka Khan - "Once You Get Started" – 4:10
- Johnny Hammond - "Fantasy" – 4:30
- Ramsey Lewis - "Whisper Zone" – 2:57
- Leon Ware - "What's Your Name" – 3:57
- Ashford & Simpson - "Stay Free" – 4:51
- Kleeer - "Tonight's the Night" – 4:43
- Dexter Wansel - "I'll Never Forget" - 4:18
- Sister Sledge - "Pretty Baby" – 3:55
- Jose Feliciano - "California Dreamin'" – 4:08
- Skyy - "Here's to You" – 4:12
- Dexter Wansel - "Life on Mars" – 5:25
- The Real Thing - "Rainin' Through My Sunshine" – 3:37
- Lalo Schifrin - "Enter The Dragon" – 2:19
- Marvin Gaye - "Here, My Dear" – 2:48
- Patrice Rushen - "Music of the Earth" – 4:00
- Brian Blessed - "The White City" – 9:31

Source (edited): "http://en.wikipedia.org/wiki/Late_Night_Tales:_Jamiroquai"

Multiquai

"**Multiquai**" is the sixth, and currently final, compilation album released by British acid jazz band Jamiroquai. The album was released in November 2006, as part of the "Multiply Your Jamiroquai" promotion, which involved the band, computer manufacturer Intel, and British computer retailer PC World. It was one of a selection of prizes issued to winners of a competition, with other prizes including tickets to an exclusive performance, "JK for Hugo", and a day's driving experience with the band. The album is only playable on a computer.

Tracklisting

- "Canned Heat" (Masters At Work Remix) - 8:25
- "Little L" (Blaze Shelter Mix) - 6:18
- "Love Foolosophy" (Lottie's Missdemeanours Vocal Mix) - 7:14
- "Emergency On Planet Earth" (Video) - 4:10
- "Cosmic Girl" (Video) - 4:00
- "Virtual Insanity" (Video) - 4:01
- "Jamiroquai On Tour" (Video) - 5:09

Source (edited): "http://en.wikipedia.org/wiki/Multiquai"

Rock Dust Light Star

Rock Dust Light Star is the seventh studio album from British funk group Jamiroquai. The album was released on November 1, 2010.

Background

The album was recorded at Jay Kay's home studio in Buckinghamshire, as well as Hook End Manor in Oxfordshire, and Karma Studios in Thailand. The album is written entirely by the band, and produced by first time collaborators Charlie Russell and Brad Spence. The band revealed that the musical style of the new album will be more centred on funk and rock, however, frontman Jay claimed that the tone and style of the album were hard for him to describe. Three singles have already been picked from the album: *White Knuckle Ride*, which was released on October 31, 2010; *Blue Skies*, which was released the following day on November 1; and *Lifeline*, which is due for release on January 24, 2011. Videos for the first two singles were premiered on September 25, 2010, via the group's official YouTube account. On October 1, a video posted on the band's new website revealed a selection of tracks that could possibly appear on the album. However, none of the three tracks, entitled "*All Mixed Up In You*", "*I've Been Working*" and "*Super Highway*", have been included on the final tracklisting. Upon the album being made available to pre-order, several retail websites claimed that the album would include a further track, entitled "*Your Window Is A Crazy Television*". It is currently unknown when or if the song will be released. Promotion of the album began on October 7, with a press conference involving band members Jay Kay, Derrick McKenzie, Sola Akingbola, Matt Johnson, Paul Turner and Rob Harris. They announced that the group were to play two concerts, in Colombia and Brazil, to promote the album, before discussing plans for a possible world tour in 2011. On October 17, 30 second-snippets of the album were made available to download free of charge from iTunes. In a review for the Daily Telegraph, the album was described as "blistering, poetic, meaty, reflective and inspiring". A total of 40 songs were recorded for the album, however, only fifteen have currently been released. The album debuted at number 7 in the UK album chart.

In Spring 2011 Jamiroquai will promote the album with a European tour, starting with Hallenstadion in Zurich on 18 March 2011, and ending with SE&CC in Glasgow on 20 April 2011.

Sales

The album debuted at number 7 in the UK with 34,378 copies sold, less than half than their previous album, Dynamite, which sold 64,150 copies in its first week in 2005. Globally, the album sold 100,000 copies in the first week of its release. As of December 4, Rock Dust Light Star has sold 211,000 copies worldwide (except in the United States, where it has not yet been released), before slipping off the Global Chart the next week. The album has been certified Gold status in the UK for passing 100,000 sales.

Tracklisting

Standard Edition/Vinyl Edition

- "Rock Dust Light Star" - 4:39 (Kay/Harris/Johnson)
- "White Knuckle Ride" - 3:33 (Kay/Johnson)
- "Smoke And Mirrors" - 4:30 (Kay/Harris/Johnson)
- "All Good In The Hood" - 3:35 (Kay/Harris/Turner)
- "Hurtin'" - 4:15 (Kay/Harris)
- "Blue Skies" - 3:51 (Kay/Johnson)
- "Lifeline" - 4:39 (Kay/Harris/Johnson)
- "She's A Fast Persuader" - 5:16 (Kay/Harris/McKenzie/Johnson/Turner/Akingbola)
- "Two Completely Different Things" - 4:25 (Kay/Harris)
- "Goodbye To My Dancer" - 4:06 (Kay/Harris/Johnson)
- "Never Gonna Be Another" - 4:08 (Kay/Johnson)
- "Hey Floyd" - 5:09 (Kay/McKenzie/Johnson/Akingbola/Turner)
- "That's Not The Funk I Want" - 3:25 - (Japanese Bonus Track)

Deluxe Edition Extra Tracks

- "All Good In The Hood" (Acoustic Version) - 3:39
- "Angeline" - 3:29
- "Hang It Over" - 4:50
- "Rock Dust Light Star" (Live at Paleo) - 5:42
- "White Knuckle Ride" (Alan Braxe Remix) - 3:17
- "Blue Skies" (Fred Falke Remix) - 4:08

Personnel

- Vocals: Jay Kay
- Drums: Derrick McKenzie
- Percussion: Sola Akingbola
- Guitar: Rob Harris
- Keyboards: Matt Johnson
- Bass: Paul Turner
- Background vocals: Hazel Fernandez & Valerie Etienne
- Saxes & flute: James Russell
- Saxes: Jim Corry
- Trumpet & flugel: Malcolm Strachan

- Strings: Simon Hale

Source (edited): "http://en.wikipedia.org/wiki/Rock_Dust_Light_Star"

Synkronized

Synkronized is the fourth studio album by Jamiroquai. Released in 1999, the album contains funk, disco, and acid jazz elements. It is also known for being the last Jamiroquai album featuring its more traditional lineup and sound.

Album information

The song "Canned Heat", which was released as the lead single from the album, is the opening track. "Where Do We Go from Here?" rocks with a leap-frogging blues piano and tangy bongoes. The album's grand finale, "King for a Day", is a regal rock-operatic excursion embellished with fully orchestrated piano and strings. The lyrics in "King for a Day" are written about Stuart Zender, Jamiroquai's bass player for their first three albums, who left the band during the making of *Synkronized*. It is noticeable that there is no bass guitar or bass synth sound in "King for a Day".

Recording sessions for the album began with Zender installed on bass, but he left partway through the recording in mid-1998, and rather than credit Zender for the tracks he had played on (and possibly co-written), Jay Kay decided to scrap all the tracks and start again. Clips of two of these tracks were shown on MTV and have been bootlegged, although not in their full form. The clips display a much more Latin/fusion sound than the songs that made it on the final album cut. Another outtake from *Synkronized* is known, called "Snooze You Lose". The song was later released on a promo CD single called "An Online Odyssey".

The bass on the album is either played on a synth bass, or by new recruit Nick Fyffe, in a style that is basically an imitation of the departed Zender. Didgeridoo player Wallis Buchanan made his last appearance in Jamiroquai, in the song "Supersonic".

Reception

- *Rolling Stone* (8–22 July 1999, pp. 144–145) - 3 Stars (out of 5) - "Synkronized is fifty minutes of sleek, sexy fun, a party album delivered with something like conviction. It's not exactly irresistible, but, really, what's the point of resisting it?"
- *Spin* (August 1999, p. 154) - 6 (out of 10) - "...redirects the band's British tendency toward smoothed-out old black jams....soaring strings, gyrating congas, hell-bent wah-wah's, and an undeniably live rhythm section that'll hustle your muscles and make you freak to the beat..."
- *Entertainment Weekly* (11 June 1999, pp. 63–4) - "Imagine if [Stevie Wonder] had made a disco album in 1977!....Synkronized is a hat trick done with the sharpest chapeau in the store." - Rating: B-
- *College Music Journal* (7 June 1999, p. 5) - "This incessantly upbeat expedition travels into the regions of Travolta-era disco...feverish funk...and instrumental iridescence...keeping your ears tuned to their funktastic audio adventures."
- *Mojo* (July 1999, p. 100) - "Synkronized proves Jamiroquai...are capable of knocking up fluid and thrilling grooves at the drop of an enormous hat....Jay's voice is wonderful throughout, delivering his admittedly toe-curling lyrics with...conviction."
- *Q* magazine (January 2000, p. 85) - Included in *Q*'s "50 Best Albums of 1999".
- "Canned Heat" – 5:31 (Kay)
- "Planet Home" – 4:44 (Kay/Smith)
- "Black Capricorn Day" – 5:41 (Kay)
- "Soul Education" – 4:15 (Kay/Smith)
- "Falling" – 3:45 (Kay/Smith)
- "Destitute Illusions" – 5:40 (Kay/Smith/McKenzie)
- "Supersonic" – 5:15 (Kay)
- "Butterfly" – 4:28 (Kay/Smith)
- "Where Do We Go from Here?" – 5:13 (Kay)
- "King for a Day" – 3:40 (Kay/Smith)
- "Deeper Underground" – 4:46
- "Get Funky" – 5:35 (Japanese bonus track)
- "Wolf in Sheep's Clothing" – 4:00 (Australian bonus track)

Source (edited): "http://en.wikipedia.org/wiki/Synkronized"

The Return of the Space Cowboy

The Return Of The Space Cowboy is the second album by the band Jamiroquai. Released in 1994, it is usually classified under the acid-jazz and funk genre.

Album information

This album has become somewhat uncommon in the United States but remains a classic in the United Kingdom and elsewhere. Many consider it to be the best and most refined example of the unique Jamiroquai sound. The album has sold 4,000,000 copies to date. Bassist Stuart Zender does not appear on the album version of the song "Space Cowboy", but does appear on the single version, and the "Stoned Again Mix".

Zender's explanation of the events which led to his non-appearance on the title track refer to a situation that occurred during the last stages of the album recording. Jay Kay informed Zender that he wanted to record a new version of the title track (the single version had already been recorded and released). However Zender had scheduled some time off to patch up his relationship with model Milla Jovovich. Kay gave his blessing to take the time off, but when Zender returned he found that Kay had recruited a session bassist, known only as "Mr X", to play on the song. Mr X is credited on the liner notes. The track "Morning Glory" was sampled in "Bite Our Style (Interlude)", a track by Missy Elliott from her album, *Supa Dupa Fly*. A similar occurrence occurred with "Manifest Destiny", sampled in "Who Do U Believe In", a track by Tupac from his album *Better Dayz*.

Track 10, "Morning Glory", was originally to be named a single, but the release was cancelled for unknown reasons. The only trace of the cancelled release lies in the US-only promo release of the single, which is a rare one nowadays. The release itself is the 'holy grail' of collecting for many fans, since two more tracks aside from the album version appear on the promo. The tracklisting of the promo itself is:

- Morning Glory (Instrumental) - 4:25
- Morning Glory (Edit) - 4:18
- Stillness In Time - 4:14

Reception

- *Rolling Stone* (23 March 1995, p. 125) - 3.5 Stars (out of 5) - "Jason Kay is a wonderfully nimble singer with a Stevie Wonder jones, and Jamiroquai parlay jazzy soul pop so tight it crackles....Nowadays, when most funk comes out of cans, Jamiroquai's live spark glows."
- *Entertainment Weekly* (10 March 1995, p. 68) - "No idle nostalgia broker, Jamiroquai is a funk-making machine with a bright future in the past." - Rating: B+
- *Q* magazine (February 2002, p. 122) - 3 stars out of 5 - "An ebullient follow-up to his storming debut."
- *The Source* (April 1995, p. 84) - "The Return Of The Space Cowboy is a mixture of acid jazz-like keyboards with an overlay of bright horns and hard basslines....This group may still be light years ahead of the hip-hop world."
- *Musician* (June 1995, p. 76) - "...sounds like a bastard spawn of Stevie Wonder and Mandrill with its vintage keyboards, jazz harmonies and fondness for rambling, jam-oriented arrangements..."

Track listing

- "Just Another Story" (Jason Kay, Toby Smith) – 8:48
- "Stillness in Time" (Jason Kay, Toby Smith) – 4:15
- "Half the Man" (Jason Kay, Toby Smith) – 4:48
- "Light Years" (Jason Kay, Toby Smith) – 5:53
- "Manifest Destiny" (Jason Kay, Toby Smith) – 6:19
- "The Kids" (Jason Kay, Toby Smith) – 5:08
- "Mr. Moon" (Jason Kay, Stuart Zender, Toby Smith) – 5:28
- "Scam" (Jason Kay, Stuart Zender) – 7:00
- "Journey to Arnhemland" (Instrumental) (Jason Kay, Toby Smith, Wallis Buchanan) – 5:19
- "Morning Glory" (Jason Kay) – 6:21
- "Space Cowboy" (Jason Kay) – 6:25
- "Light Years" (Live Version) (Jason Kay, Toby Smith) – 5:53 (US Bonus Track)
- "Space Cowboy" (Classic Radio Mix) (Jason Kay) - 4:59 (Mexican Bonus Track)
- "Space Cowboy" (Stoned Again Mix) (Jason Kay) - 7:58 (Japanese Bonus Track)

Singles

- "The Kids" - March 21, 1994
- "Space Cowboy" - September 26, 1994
- "Half the Man" - November 7, 1994
- "Stillness In Time" - June 19, 1995
- "Light Years" - September 6, 1995

Outtakes

- "Do That Dance" - Played several times during live performances. The most notable performances were at Club Citta, on December 10, 1993, in Tokyo, Japan, and in Milan, Italy, on December 5, 1993.
- "Life Goes On" - A track, which was later merged together with "Do That Dance" to create "Scam"
- "Let Me Believe" - An original version of "Manifest Destiny", performed live in Milan in December 1993
- "The Kids Got Funky Soul" - An outtake from the band's debut album, adapted to create "The Kids"

Songs For Manitu

A live recording of the band in Milan, Italy, on December 5, 1993, was released on a Limited Edition live album, entitled "Songs For Manitu". It was the group's first live album, of which only 500 copies were produced.. Released in February 1995, the release includes many of the "Outtakes" from Return of the Space Cowboy, as well as two further original tracks not included on any other release.

Tracklisting

- "Blow Your Mind" - 8:52
- "Didgin' Out" - 4:09
- "God Made Me Funky" - 6:04
- "Let Me Believe" - 6:56
- "When You Gonna Learn" - 6:41
- "Life Goes On" - 5:02
- "Do That Dance" - 8:32
- "Emergency On Planet Earth" - 4:01
- "Too Young To Die" - 4:51
- "Rock The House" - 7:56
- "Signed, Sealed, Delivered" - 2:46
- "Stu's Tune" - 9:40

Source (edited): "http://en.wikipedia.org/wiki/The_Return_of_the_Space_Cowboy"

Travelling Without Moving

Travelling Without Moving is the third album by Jamiroquai. Released in 1996, the album features the international hit single "Virtual Insanity".

The album also has a more diverse sound than previous albums, with more instrumental tracks, and a greater electronic influence, evident in songs such as "Alright", which mixed new synthetic sounds with shades of acid-jazz.

Album information

Around this time, Jay Kay's love of sportscars reached a peak, as reflected by the Ferrari-esque logo adorning the album cover and engine noises on the title track. This led some to accuse him of selling out on the environmentalist message of his previous albums.

The title track "Travelling Without Moving" appropriately introduces a new high-octane sound which features strongly in later albums. This is also the last album with bassist Stuart Zender.

The RIAA certified *Travelling Without Moving* Platinum on 3 November 1997, denoting 1 million shipments in the United States - this is the only RIAA certification the band has ever obtained.

The sales of *Travelling Without Moving* are estimated to about 11.5 million units sold worldwide, which makes it the best-selling funk album of all time. The large number of copies sold was helped by the success of the "Virtual Insanity" music video, which won a Grammy Award and 4 MTV Awards. The album went 3× Platinum album in the United Kingdom, and was certified platinum by the RIAA in the United States.

With the success of *Travelling Without Moving*, Jamiroquai's popularity had increased considerably and influenced fans to listen to past releases. "Virtual Insanity" became the one of the first videos by Jamiroquai to reach America with the help of MTV (BET, Black Entertainment Television, had broadcasted less popular videos previously), and the name "Jamiroquai" became known worldwide.

Q magazine (10/96, p. 164) - 4 Stars (out of 5) - "Tighter and more compact in its production that the epic funk arrangements of...The Return of the Space Cowboy....no-one with ears can deny Jason Kay's musicality--he's an extraordinary singer, and proves it here."

The Source (2/97, p. 86) - "Travelling is essentially about the metaphysics of having a good time....Jamiroquai have a thousand musical tricks up their sleeves; edgy horns laced with jazz intricacies, energetic bass lines and disco rhythms."

Source (edited): "http://en.wikipedia.org/wiki/Travelling_Without_Moving"

John Thirkell

John Thirkell (aka **Johnny Thirkell**) is a British trumpet and flugelhorn player, who has appeared on hundreds of pop, rock, and jazz recordings. Through the 1980s and early 1990s he was on at least one album in the UK Charts continuously, without a break, for over 13 years. In 2009 he had two consecutive UK No.1 singles with Pixie Lott and was the first person to be inducted into the Musician's Union "Hall of Fame"

He is perhaps best known for playing with Level 42, in partnership with fellow British session musician, saxophonist Gary Barnacle, - known as The Phantom Horns.

His other credits include work with artists such as George Michael, Jamiroquai, UB40, Cher, Tina Turner, Pet Shop Boys, Swing Out Sister and many more, along with stints in the Buddy Rich Orchestra and Gil Evans Orchestra.

John Thirkell is currently a co-owner and director of music venture PureSolo.

Credits

- Level 42 Forever Now (Resurgent) *Group Member*
- Level 42 Guaranteed - *Group Member*
- Jamiroquai Emergency on Planet Earth - *Trumpet, Horn Arrangements*
- Jamiroquai Bad Girls Live - *Trumpet*
- Jamiroquai Return of the Space Cowboy - *Trumpet, Horn Arrangements*
- George Michael Older - *Flugelhorn, Upper Flugelhorn & Trumpet*
- UB40 Labour of Love II - *Trumpet*
- Swing Out Sister Breakout - *Trumpet*
- Swing Out Sister Surrender - *Trumpet*
- Tina Turner Simply the Best - *Trumpet*
- Jools Holland World of His Own - *Trumpet*
- Phil Collins Prince's Trust Concert 1987 & 2010 - *Trumpet, Flugelhorn*
- Nacha Pop El Momento (Re-Edition)
- Various Artists Heart of Innocence - Status Quo Don't Stop: 30th Anniversary Album - *Trumpet, Flugelhorn*
- Westlife My Girl - *Trumpet*
- Westlife What Becomes of the Broken Hearted - *Trumpet*
- Lisa Stansfield Lisa Stanfield - *Horn Arrangements, Trumpet*
- Lisa Stansfield Swing (Original Soundtrack) - *Trumpet*
- Queen Princes Trust 2010 - *Trumpet/Flugelhorn*
- Kylie Minogue Fever - *Flute, Trumpet*
- Kylie Minogue Let's Get To It - *Trumpet*
- Kylie Minogue Better the Devil You Know - *Trumpet*
- Tom Jones Reload) - *Flugelhorn, Trumpet*
- Spandau Ballet Heart Like a Sky - *Trumpet, Flugelhorn*
- M People Bizarre Fruit - *Trumpet, Flugelhorn*
- Prefab Sprout Jordan: The Comeback - *Trumpet, Flugelhorn*
- Frankie Goes to Hollywood Liverpool - *Trumpet, Flugelhorn*
- Take That Nobody Else - *Trumpet*
- ABC Lexicon of Love - *Trumpet, Flugelhorn*
- Roger Waters Radio Kaos - *Trumpet, Flugelhorn*
- Bros Changing Faces - *Trumpet*
- Eric Clapton Prince's Trust Concert 1987 & 2010 - *Trumpet, Flugelhorn*
- Stereo MC's Connected - *Trumpet*
- Randy Crawford Rich & Poor - *Trumpet*
- Katrina and the Waves Walking on Sunshine - *Trumpet*
- Natalie Imbruglia Satellite - *Trum-*

- pet, Flugelhorn
- Culture Club Your Kisses Are Charity - *Trumpet*
- The Style Council Have You Ever Had It Blue - *Trumpet*
- Lionel Richie Renaissance - *Trumpet, Flugelhorn*
- Cavern Sound The Beatles Greatest Hits - *Producer*
- The The Infected (Sony Reissue) - *Trumpet*
- The The Dusk (Sony Reissue) - *Trumpet*
- Anastacia One Day in Your Life (Import Single) -
- Cher Living Proof (Japan Bonus Track) - *Flugelhorn, Trumpet*
- George Harrison Princes Trust Concert 1987 - *Trumpet, Flugelhorn*
- Ringo Starr Princes Trust Concert 1987 - *Trumpet, Flugelhorn*
- Miriam Stockley Second Nature - *Trumpet*
- Various Artists Do the Right Thing (Soundtrack Bonus Tracks) -
- Swing Out Sister Live at the Jazz Cafe - *Flugelhorn, Trumpet*
- Byron Stingily Club Stories (Import Bonus Tracks) -
- Culture Club Don't Mind If I Do - *Trumpet*
- Jakko Jakszyk The Road to Ballina - *Trumpet*
- Tom Jones Reload - *Trumpet*
- Maxi Priest CombiNation - *Trumpet*
- Dany Brillant Nouveau Jour - *Arranger, Trumpet*
- Tina Turner Wildest Dreams - *Trumpet*
- M People Fresco - *Trumpet*
- Various Artists Doctor Who: Downtime Vocals
- Warren Shaw Other Side of Midnight - *Horn, Trumpet*
- Right Said Fred Smashing! - *Trumpet*
- Angélique Kidjo Fifa - *Trumpet*
- Kiko Veneno Esta Muy Bien Eso Del Carino - *Trumpet*
- Angélique Kidjo Aye - *Trumpet*
- Swing Out Sister Living Return - *Flugelhorn, Trumpet*
- Dorado Dorado: The Gold Sessions - *Trumpet*
- Alejandro Sanz Si Tu Me Miras - *Trumpet*
- Various Artists Dorado: A Compilation - *Trumpet*
- Pet Shop Boys Very - *Conductor, Brass*
- Pet Shop Boys Relentless - *Brass*
- Clive Griffin Clive Griffin - *Trumpet*
- Isabel Pantoja Corazon Herido - *Trumpet*
- Swing Out Sister Get in Touch with Yourself - *Flugelhorn, Trumpet*
- Diesel Hepfidelity - *Trumpet*
- 29 Palms Fatal Joy - *Flugelhorn, Trumpet*
- Big Dish Satellites - *Trumpet*
- Wop Bop Torledo Wop Bop Torledo - *Trumpet*
- The Beautiful South Welcome to the Beautiful South - *Flugelhorn, Trumpet*
- The Beautiful South Carry On Up the Charts - *Flugelhorn, Trumpet*
- The Sugarcubes Here Today, Tomorrow Next Week! - *Trumpet*
- Jimmy Somerville Read My Lips - *Trumpet*
- Tony Banks Bankstatement - *Trumpet*
- Randy Crawford Rich and Poor - *Brass*
- Clive Griffin Step by Step - *Overdubs*
- Various Artists Do the Right Thing (Soundtrack) - *Trumpet*
- Toni Childs Union - *Horn*
- Hothouse Flowers People - *Brass*
- Was (Not Was) What Up, Dog? - *Brass, Overdubs*
- Do Re Mi The Happiest Place in Town - *Trumpet*
- Big Dish Creeping up on Jesus - *Trumpet*
- Grace Jones Slave to the Rhythm - *Percussion, Trumpet*
- Elaine Paige Stages - *Flugelhorn*
- Pixie Lott Mama Do - *Trumpet*
- Pixie Lott Boys & Girls - *Trumpet*
- James Morrison 'Songs For You, Truths For Me' - *Trumpet & Flugelhorn*
- Kiri Te Kanawa 'World in Union' - *Trumpet*
- Jamie Cullum - Princes Trust 2010
- Paloma Faith - Princes Trust 2010

Source (edited): "http://en.wikipedia.org/wiki/John_Thirkell"

Matt Johnson (keyboardist)

Matt Johnson is a keyboardist who plays for the alternative jazz band Jamiroquai.

Matt was aged one and a half when he started playing the piano at his family home. 'My dad was a musician so there was always music playing in the house, but I remember being taught by a scary old piano teacher, who must have been over 90 years old'. His influences range from Herbie Hancock and Miles Davis through to Squarepusher.

Before playing in Jamiroquai he was a hugely respected writer and performer in bands "Sunray", with whom Kym Mazelle recorded a cover of "Perhaps", and Nu Hope. He has also written and produced artists with artists such as Alexia, who had a minor hit with "Ring".

His route into Jamiroquai was via an audition in 2001. He was recommended by Simon Katz, a previous guitarist, and Derrick gave him the call. The audition was a success and Matt is now a well established writer and member of the Jamiroquai family.

Johnson has recently become chief song writing partner and producer along with fellow band mate, guitarist Rob Harris, for the highly anticipated teenage singer/songwriter Julian Perretta (Sony BMG) towards his debut album. A date for release is thought to be 2009.

Source (edited): "http://en.wikipedia.org/wiki/Matt_Johnson_(keyboardist)"

Mike Smith (saxophonist)

Mike Smith is an English musician. He is an arranger, composer, conductor, studio musician, and keyboardist, but specializes in saxophone.

Smith studied jazz and contemporary music at the Leeds College of Music, from which he graduated in 1988. He went on to Guildhall School of Music, to attain his post graduate certificate in jazz and rock.

He gained experience as a studio musician, playing and touring with Brand New Heavies and Jamiroquai. As an arranger and conductor he also worked with Marc Almond, David Cassidy and Laura Michelle Kelly.

In the recent years Smith worked closely with Damon Albarn, contributing to Gorillaz, Blur's *Think Tank*, and Albarn's Mali Music Project.

Smith is currently in the band The Ailerons, with Blur drummer Dave Rowntree.

Source (edited): "http://en.wikipedia.org/wiki/Mike_Smith_(saxophonist)"

Nick Fyffe

Nick Fyffe (born 14 October 1972, Reading, England) is an English bassist, known for being an ex-bassist of British funk band Jamiroquai. He replaced Stuart Zender in 1999 with the release of the album *Synkronized*. He was in the process of applying to a Jamiroquai tribute band, when he got the offer to join Jamiroquai. Fyffe recorded and toured with the band until his departure in 2003.

Since his departure from Jamiroquai, Fyffe has been lecturing at various colleges, and played with the UK dance ensemble, The Shapeshifters. In 2006, 2007 and 2008 Fyffe took part in 'The Sunflower Jam', an annual live music charity event. Since the first event in 2006, he has played alongside Robert Plant, Deep Purple, Status Quo, and Bruce Dickinson.

He is an alumnus from Chichester College. He is related to the early 20th century entertainer, Will Fyffe.

In October 2009, Fyffe was picked to join thenewno2 (members Dhani Harrison, Jeremy Faccone, Jonathan Sadoff, and touring drummer Frank Zummo) on their US tour with the Australian rock band, Wolfmother.

Fyffe played on thenewno2's first album, *You Are Here*, along with Harrison and fellow founding member Oliver Hecks.

Source (edited): "http://en.wikipedia.org/wiki/Nick_Fyffe"

Stuart Zender

Stuart Patrick Jude Zender (born 18 March 1974, Sheffield, South Yorkshire) is an English bassist, songwriter and record producer. He is best known for being the original bass player for Jamiroquai.

Early life

Raised in Philadelphia, he attended Leighton Park School in Reading (for a year in 1988-89 before being expelled) known for its strength in music. He lived in a lower middle class family. Stuart left his home when he was seventeen. Before he left, his mother gave him two thousand pounds that she saved, to give Stuart a head start with things in life. As Stuart said, he never had good business acumen, so instead of investing that money in some way, he went to the music store and bought a Warwick Streamer bass (which cost nearly the whole amount given to him by his mother). Before picking up a Warwick, Stuart played a Music Man Stingray bass. Of his early bands, the most famous was prank rock group Fabulous. The 1991 outfit were chiefly made up of NME writers and photographers.

Jamiroquai

Stuart was one of the founding members of the highly-acclaimed funk/acid band Jamiroquai. He joined the band in 1993, and instantly became highly approved by the audiences for his playing style. Soon after, Zender was asked to become an official Warwick basses endorser. Zender received a number of unique custom shop Streamer models. He played, co-wrote and produced on Jamiroquai's first three albums: *Emergency on Planet Earth*, *The Return of the Space Cowboy* and *Travelling Without Moving*. According to the Guinness World Records, Travelling Without Moving is the best selling funk album of all time and currently has sold around 11.5 million records worldwide. Zender left Jamiroquai during recording of their fourth album Synkronized because of conflicts with lead singer Jay Kay. The circumstances behind his departure have never been fully revealed, but Stuart explained that he felt that he (and other band members) were not being credited for assisting in songwriting and producing. He also stated that he tendered his resignation to spend more time with his budding family. Stuart was replaced by Nick Fyffe, who had previously been in a Jamiroquai tribute band. Fyffe left in 2003 and was later replaced by Paul Turner in 2005.

Post-Jamiroquai (1998-present)

After Jamiroquai, Zender had his own project called "AZUR" which signed a record deal with Virgin US. However the project was shelved and was then available on the internet for a short time. He has also worked with numerous artists, including All Saints, Omar, Lauryn Hill, Gorillaz, Samuel Purdey, Ms. Dynamite and Stevie Wonder. He also dated singer Melanie Blatt of former UK girl group All Saints. The two were together for seven years. They have one daughter together, named Lilyella. Some of Stuart's most recent work has been with his latest band "LEROI". They were signed onto Geffen Records in Los Angeles. The deal fell through after the heads of the company, Polly Anthony and Jordan Shurr, who signed them, were made redundant. Zender left Los Angeles in the summer of 2006 to become the Musical director and bass player for Mark Ronson. The release of the album *Version* in 2007 proved to be a larger success than first expected. Thanks to the success he has performed with Ronson at numerous popular events such as "Radio 1's Big Weekend", "O2 Wireless at Hyde Park", "Global Gathering" and "Glastonbury", and festivals all over Europe including "Montreux Jazz Festival" in Switzerland and "North Sea Jazz Festival" in The Hague. They were also recently special guests on Jay Z's UK tour.

On September 26, 2009, Zender finally broke his silence on his departure from Jamiroquai on the *Cool Lounge* radio show. While going through the motions of heartache, Zender says that he then became quiet and introverted which his band mates mistook for vanity. "Jay actually called me a Prima Donna at one point I remember. And I was like, 'that's weird coming from you, mate!' " Zender says that throughout the hard times he looks back on his time with Jamiroquai with fond memories.

Recently, Zender has just set up his own record label "White Buffalo Recordings" and has started working on new material for his own album.

Zender and Warwick have recently reunited to produce a Stuart Zender signature bass guitar. Zender began his career by playing Warwick guitars in 1993, when Jamiroquai was formed. All bass players wanted to know what was behind the funky bass lines that became the defining essence of Jamiroquai's music. TV appearances and magazine interviews followed revealing Warwick as the basses used. An endorsement soon followed along with many designs - the Iroquai "rug" bass, the all white bass including blue LEDs, the Chrome "Ender" along with many of the original basses used.

- 1x Warwick SZ Signature Bass 4-string
- 1x Warwick SZ Signature Bass 4-string (Red one, saw live in Paris for Mark Ronson)
- 1x Warwick "Iroquai Rug Bass" Streamer 5-string
- 1x Warwick "The Chrome Ender Bass" Streamer Stage I 4-string
- 1x Fender 1964 Precision Bass
- 1x Warwick Streamer Stage II 5-string (used in 1995 live)
- 1x Alembic Epic 4-string (onstage backup bass)
- Warwick Amplification

Album appearances

- Jamiroquai - *Emergency on Planet Earth* (bass)
- Jamiroquai - *The Return of the Space Cowboy* (bass, writer)
- Guru - Jazzmatazz, Vol. 2: The New Reality *(bass)*
- Jamiroquai - *Travelling Without Moving* (bass, writer)
- *Live from 6A - Late Night With Conan O'Brien*
- *Lauryn Hill - The Miseducation of Lauryn Hill*
- *Mica Paris - Black Angel* (bass)
- *Now Dance 98 - Compilation.* (bass)
- *Omar - Best by Far* (Bass, Percussion, Electric Guitar, Keyboards, Programming, Co-Writer, Producer)
- *All Saints - Saints and Sinners* (Writer, Producer, Mixer, Keyboards, Bass, Percussion, Strings, Programming)
- Space Monkeyz vs. Gorillaz - *Laika Come Home*
- Mark Ronson - *Version* (bass)

Video appearances

- Jamiroquai - When You Gonna Learn
- Jamiroquai - Blow Your Mind
- Jamiroquai - Emergency on Planet Earth
- Jamiroquai - Light Years
- Jamiroquai - Stillness in Time
- Jamiroquai - Space Cowboy
- Jamiroquai - Cosmic Girl
- Jamiroquai - Alright
- Jamiroquai - High Times
- Jamiroquai - Virtual Insanity
- Ms. Dynamite - Dy-Na-Mi-Tee
- Mark Ronson - Oh My God (Feat. Lily Allen)
- Mark Ronson - Valerie (Feat. Amy Winehouse)
- US TV Appearance - Stop Me - Conan O'Brien, NBC, 2007.07.12

Source (edited): "http://en.wikipedia.org/wiki/Stuart_Zender"

Toby Smith

Toby Smith (born **Toby Grafftey-Smith**, 29 October 1970, London) is a musician, most famous for being the keyboardist and co-songwriter for Jamiroquai from 1992 up to 2001.

Contrary to popular opinion, which gives much of the credit to Jay Kay, Smith was in fact the musical and lyrical genius behind all of Jamiroquai's biggest songs, such as "Emergency on Planet Earth", "Virtual Insanity", "Alright", "Blow Your Mind", "Deeper Underground", "Do You Know Where You're Coming From?", "Half the Man" and "High Times"..

He is the current music producer and manager for the English indie pop band, The Hoosiers.

Source (edited): "http://en.wikipedia.org/wiki/Toby_Smith"

(Don't) Give Hate a Chance

"(Don't) Give Hate A Chance" is the third and final single from British Acid Jazz band Jamiroquai's sixth studio album, *Dynamite*. The song was written by Jason Kay, Rob Harris and Matt Johnston. It was produced by Kay and Mike Spencer. The single was released on November 7, 2005, peaking on the UK Singles Chart at #27.

Tracklisting
UK CD1
- "Don't Give Hate A Chance"
- "Don't Give Hate A Chance" (Steve Mac Classic Remix Radio Edit)

UK CD2
- "Don't Give Hate A Chance"
- "Don't Give Hate A Chance" (Steve Mac Classic Remix)
- "Don't Give Hate A Chance" (Freemasons Remix)

Music Video

The Buffalo Man in the animated music video for the song.

The video for "(Don't) Give Hate a Chance" is Jamiroquai's first-ever computer animated music video and pays homage to the Italian cartoon *La Linea*. To promote the release of the video, Sony BMG organised the video to be projected on a number of outdoor venues around central London, including the walls of the Chelsea Barracks military grounds and a car park in the Soho district. A replacement to the original video appeared in late October, which included changes such as the ground being replaced by plants and rocks and significant changes to the final minute of the video. The title of the song is a reference to the song "Give Peace a Chance" by John Lennon.

Source (edited): "http://en.wikipedia.org/wiki/(Don%27t)_Give_Hate_a_Chance"

Alright (Jamiroquai song)

"**Alright**" is the third single from British Acid Jazz band Jamiroquai's third studio album, *Travelling Without Moving*. The song was written by Jay Kay. The song peaked at #6 on the UK Singles Chart. It is the group's only single to chart on the U.S. *Billboard* Hot 100. The group recorded an updated version of the song for their 2006 greatest hits compilation.

Track listing
UK CD1 (664235 2)
- "Alright" (Radio Edit) – 3:39
- "Alright" (Vocal Version) – 6:04
- "Alright" (Dub-Vocal) – 5:34
- "Alright" (DJ Version Excursion) – 6:47

UK CD2 (664235 5)
- "Alright" (Full Length Version) – 4:23
- "Alright" (Tee's In House Mix) – 7:20
- "Alright" (Tee's Digital Club) – 7:15
- "Alright" (Tee's Radio Jay) – 3:27

Music video
The music video takes place at a party. Jay Kay is filmed singing while in an elevator with the rest of Jamiroquai. Then, they play at a party and the end scene is live footage from Argentina. The video starts as a sequel of Cosmic Girl, with Jamiroquai appearing in sports cars, and Kay driving the same Lamborghini.

Source (edited): "http://en.wikipedia.org/wiki/Alright_(Jamiroquai_song)"

An Online Odyssey

"**An Online Odyssey**" is a promotional only album released by British Acid Jazz group Jamiroquai. The album was released in the United Kingdom in the Summer of 2001, to promote the launch of "A Funk Odyssey", as well as the band's new website. Around 10,000 copies of the album were pressed, with most being distrubted in Britain. British copies of the album also featured a membership postcard for the group's fan club, "A Club Odyssey".

Tracklisting
- "Black Capricorn Day" (White Knights Remix) - 7:38
- "Snooze, You Lose" - 3:55
- "Black Capricorn Day" (Video) - 3:42

Source (edited): "http://en.wikipedia.org/wiki/An_Online_Odyssey"

Blow Your Mind (Jamiroquai song)

"**Blow Your Mind**" is the third single from Jamiroquai's debut studio album, *Emergency on Planet Earth*. The single was released on June 4, 1993, peaking at #17 on the UK Singles Chart. The single was also featured on the group's Greatest Hits album, however, in a very edited form. Like both of the group's previous singles, two versions of the song exist: a heavily edited radio edit, running at 3:51, and the full-length album version, running at 8:35. The latter version has only ever been included on the group's debut album release. All other releases which include the track include the radio version.

Tracklisting
UK CD Single
- "Blow Your Mind" (Radio Edit) - 3:51
- "Blow Your Mind" (Parts 1 & 2) - 8:35
- "Hooked Up" - 4:36
- "When You Gonna Learn" (JK Mix) - 6:20

Source (edited): "http://en.wikipedia.org/wiki/Blow_Your_Mind_(Jamiroquai_song)"

Blue Skies (Jamiroquai song)

"**Blue Skies**" is the second single from British alternative group Jamiroquai's studio album, *Rock Dust Light Star*. The single was released via Digital Download on November 1, 2010. The song was written by band frontman Jay Kay and Matt Johnson. It is the band's second single to be released under Mercury Records. The single did not receive an official physical release due to the fact it was released on the same date as the group's album. It appears that the Jamiroquai logo typeface has been stretched vertically for this release. The video for the single was made available on the group's YouTube account on September 25. The track peaked at #76 on the UK Singles Chart.

Tracklisting
Digital Download and CD Single
- "Blue Skies" - 4:02

Promotional CD Single
- "Blue Skies" (Original Mix) - 3:52
- "Blue Skies" (Linus Loves Remix) - 7:30
- "Blue Skies" (Flux Pavilion Remix) - 5:46
- "Blue Skies" (Fred Falke Remix) - 7:48
- "Blue Skies" (Fred Falke Instrumental) - 7:40
- "Blue Skies" (Fred Falke Radio Edit) - 4:08

Music video
The music video shows Jay Kay riding a Harley Davidson motorbike through the outback of Australia, attempting to find a beauty spot where he can look at the Blue Skies, hence the title of the song. The video tracks his journey to and from the spot, and also shows Jay reminiscing about his time with the band.

Source (edited): "http://en.wikipedia.org/wiki/Blue_Skies_(Jamiroquai_song)"

Canned Heat (song)

"**Canned Heat**" is the second single from British Acid Jazz band Jamiroquai's fourth studio album, *Synkronized*, released in 1999. The song was their second #1 on the U.S. Dance Chart and peaked at #4 on the UK Singles Chart. The music video was directed by Jonas Åkerlund. The song is used in the film *Napoleon Dynamite*, as background music during the title character's dance performance before a high school assembly.

Tracklisting
UK CD1 (667302 2)
- "Canned Heat" (7" Edit) – 3:46
- "Canned Heat" (Radio Edit) – 3:19
- "Wolf In Sheep's Clothing" – 4:00

UK CD2 (667302 5)
- "Canned Heat" (7" Edit) – 3:46
- "Canned Heat" (Album Version) – 5:30
- "Deeper Underground" (Chillington Mix) – 6:56

Cassette (667302 4)
- "Canned Heat" (7" Edit) – 3:46
- "Wolf In Sheep's Clothing" – 4:00

Single Information
Over the numerous releases of the "Canned Heat" single, two B-Sides exist. "Wolf In Sheep's Clothing" is a funky instrumental that features an intro of two drum beats that lasts about 1.5 seconds and then enters a strongly bass driven repetitive melody. Many keyboard effects are used throughout the song's 4.00 minute duration. The song enters a percussion section at 3.07 and lasts for the remainder of the song slowly fading out from 3.45. The song can be found only on the Canned Heat single and some editions of the *Synkronized* album, the Australian double disc release being an example. Nowhere on the single or in the music notes of editions of *Synkronized* containing the song does it list who it was written or recorded by. There is a possibility that the track may be a *Synkronized* outtake that was written and recorded while Stuart Zender was still a part of the band and removed from the majority releases after it was re-recorded, or the song may have been recorded for the single. "Deeper Underground - Chillington Mix" is featured on the second release of "Canned Heat". Chillington is not the name of an artist or DJ, but the name of the studios at Jay's Home in Buckinghamshire. The Chillington Mix samples heavily from the Jamiroquai song Getinfunky which is found on some special releases of *Synkronized*, such as the Japanese release where it replaced "Deeper Underground" as the bonus track, and alongside Wolf In Sheep's Clothing on the Australian double disc. On the *High Times: The Singles* DVD, Jay comments

on a bonus feature that the original *Godzilla* song was just made of "Ominous noises" which strongly matches the sound of Getinfunky. When the title or the remix and "Ominous noises" evidence is pared it strongly suggests that "Getinfunky" is an early version of the *Godzilla* song which later evolved into "Deeper Underground".

Popular Culture

"Canned Heat" is featured in the feature film *Napoleon Dynamite*, during the title character's dance performance at the end of a high school assembly. The song is also featured in the film "Center Stage", released in 2000, in which the dancers perform a piece to this song at the end of the movie. Also, the song was used in the rhythm based Xbox 360 game *Dance Dance Revolution Universe 3*. The music video was played in the background as the song would be played. A cover of the song was featured in a level of the game Elite Beat Agents. Another cover of the song was featured in the European version of Donkey Konga.

Source (edited): "http://en.wikipedia.org/wiki/Canned_Heat_(song)"

Corner of the Earth

"**Corner Of The Earth**" is the fourth and final single from British Acid Jazz band Jamiroquai's fifth studio album, *A Funk Odyssey*. The song was written by Jason Kay. It is a bossa nova-type track, reflecting on the problems that people of the earth have to suffer. The song peaked at #31 on the UK Singles Chart and was the last Jamiroquai single to use the DVD format. It's DVD single is referred to as one of the rarest DVD singles in history, although over 100,000 copies were printed.

Track listings

UK CD1 (672788 2)
- "Corner Of The Earth" – 5:40
- "Main Vein" (Knee Deep Classic Mix) – 6:51
- "Main Vein" (Deep Swing's Jazzy Thumper Mix) – 7:21

UK CD2 (672788 5)
- "Corner Of The Earth" – 5:40
- "Bad Girls" (Live At The Brits 2002) (Feat. Anastacia) – 4:13
- "Titan" (Live At The Telewest Arena) – 3:25
- "Corner Of The Earth" (Video) - 3:54

UK DVD (672788 9)
- "Corner Of The Earth" (Video) – 3:54
- "Corner Of The Earth" (Audio) - 5:40
- "Bad Girls" (Live At The Brits 2002) (Feat. Anastacia) (Audio) – 4:13
- "Love Foolosophy" (Mondo Grosso Love Acoustic Mix) (Audio) - 4:53
- "Bad Girls" (Live At The Brits 2002) (Feat. Anastacia) (Video Clip) – 2:00

Source (edited): "http://en.wikipedia.org/wiki/Corner_of_the_Earth"

Cosmic Girl

"**Cosmic Girl**" is the second single from British Acid Jazz band Jamiroquai's third studio album, *Travelling Without Moving*. Released in November 1996, it achieved great chart success, peaking at #6 on the UK Singles Chart.

Background

While the poppy disco single, and especially it's chart performance, had received mixed reviews from critics, it has become one of the better-known tracks of the band, and a concert staple. Live versions usually last for 7 to 8 minutes, nearly double the duration of the album version. In 2006, it was reissued as part of the "Classic Club Mixes" series, which also included "Space Cowboy", "Deeper Underground", "Love Foolosophy" and "Alright". The B-side to the single was an instrumental "Slipin' 'N' Slidin'" , a rather obscure song originating from another old Jamiroquai tune called "Mr Boogie", which was a live-only song. "Slipin 'N' Slidin'", just like "Mr Boogie", also had a vocal version.

Music video

Screenshot from the music video

The video, directed by Adrian Moat, shows three famous supercars driving and racing each other through several highways and mountain roads across a desert landscape from clear day-light to dawn. The cars on the video are a black Ferrari F355 berlinetta, a purple Lamborghini Diablo SE30 and a red Ferrari F40. Jay Kay appears to be driving the purple Lamborghini with Stuart Zender on the co-pilot seat, but the drivers of the other cars are not shown in detail. It has four different edits: Versions 1-3, and the so called 'Jay's cut' version. Before filming, Jay's Diablo had to be shipped overseas for the video shoot. Apparently, the company which was hired to transport the car had a driver that was keen to drive the car. Jay let the guy drive the car, but he was involved in an accident which wrecked the car, rendering the $239,000 car completely unusable. The car that appears in the video was rented from a local collector. The F40 was provided by the Pink Floyd drummer Nick Mason, who drove in the video as well. While filming, the driver's side window in Jay Kay's Lamborghini was accidentally smashed. Due to the tight timescales involved, the video was still shot, but with the window removed. This is why Jay Kay appears to be driving around the desert late at night with his windows down. Jay Kay mentioned in an interview that the Lamborghini had its windscreen removed to aid with the filming, due to space limitations inside, and the windscreen angle from outside. The missing windscreen can be seen when the Lamborghini overtakes the black Ferrari on an uphill shot. The video was filmed at the Cabo de Gata, in Spain.

Tracklisting

UK CD1
- "Cosmic Girl" (Radio Edit) - 3:45
- "Slipin' 'N' Slidin'" – 3:36
- "Didjital Vibrations" - 5:47
- "Cosmic Girl" (Classic Radio Mix) – 4:02

UK CD2
- "Cosmic Girl" (Album Version) - 4:03
- "Cosmic Girl" (Quasar Mix) - 7:41
- "Cosmic Girl" (David Morales Classic Mix) - 9:22
- "Cosmic Girl" (Cosmic Dub) – 6:47

Cassette
- "Cosmic Girl" (Radio Edit) - 03:45
- "Slipin N' Slidin'" - 03:36

7" Single
- "Cosmic Girl" (Radio Edit) - 03:45
- "Ci Sarò" - 4:11

Source (edited): "http://en.wikipedia.org/wiki/Cosmic_Girl"

Deeper Underground

"**Deeper Underground**" is the first single from British Acid Jazz band Jamiroquai's fourth studio album, *Synkronized*, despite the track only appearing as a hidden track on the release. It was included on the soundtrack of the American film *Godzilla*, and was released as the lead single from it. The track also later appeared on the special edition of the group's fifth album *A Funk Odyssey*. It is the group's only single to have reached #1 on the UK Singles Chart.

Tracklisting

UK CD1 (666218 2)
- "Deeper Underground" (radio edit) – 3:33
- "Deeper Underground" (The Metro Mix) – 6:59
- "Deeper Underground" (instrumental) – 4:44

UK CD2 (666218 5)
- "Deeper Underground" – 4:44
- "Deeper Underground" (The Ummah Mix) – 5:01
- "Deeper Underground" (S-Man Meets Da Northface Killa Dub) – 9:02

UK 12" (665904 6)
- "Deeper Underground" (S-Man Meets Da Northface Killa Dub) – 9:02
- "Deeper Underground" (The Ummah Mix) – 5:01
- "Deeper Underground" (The Metro Mix) – 6:59
- "Deeper Underground" (radio edit) – 3:33

Music video

Directed by Mike Lipscombe, the video was used as a promotional tool for the 1998 film *Godzilla*. Partly shot on location at Grays' State Theatre, it depicts a film theatre in which the movie is being shown. However, as the screen shows Godzilla walking on the ocean floor, one of its feet breaks the screen and water floods into the theatre as if the screen were made of glass and everything behind it were real. The theatre turns into chaos as the audience tries to get out alive, in the midst of which Jay Kay appears and dances on top of the seats. Several other things go through the screen, including a helicopter and a taxi. Another version of the video replaces Godzilla with a man in the movie who smashes an aquarium, causing the theatre to flood. The rest of the video is completely identical.

Source (edited): "http://en.wikipedia.org/wiki/Deeper_Underground"

Do You Know Where You're Coming From?

"**Do You Know Where You're Coming From?**" is the lead single from British funk band Jamiroquai's third studio album, *Travelling Without Moving*. Only included as a bonus track on the album, the track features music and additional vocals by M-Beat, who also produced the track. Released on February 14, 1996, the single peaked at #14 on the UK Singles Chart. The single later appeared as a B-side to the group's following single, "Virtual Insanity".

Tracklisting

UK CD Single
- "Do You Know Where You're Coming From?" (Radio Edit - Original Mix)
- "Do You Know Where You're Coming From?" (Radio Edit - Touch Of Horn Mix)
- "Do You Know Where You're Coming From?" (Extended Mix)
- "Do You Know Where You're Coming From?" (Full Horns Mix)
- "Do You Know Where You're Coming From?" (Intelligent Groove Mix)
- "Do You Know Where You're Coming From?" (Dextrous Remix)

Source (edited): "http://en.wikipedia.org/wiki/Do_You_Know_Where_You%27re_Coming_From%3F"

Emergency on Planet Earth (song)

"**Emergency On Planet Earth**" is the fourth and final single from Jamiroquai's debut studio album *of the same name*. The song was written by Jay Kay. It has a very environmentalist tone, urging the listener to "stop modernisation going on." The track peaked at #14 on the UK Singles Chart and at #4 on the U.S. Dance Chart.

. An alternate version of the song, which uses a completely different bass track and intro, and includes some changes in the arrangements, was featured in the music video for the song. This version was only released on the group's greatest hits compilation, *High Times: Singles 1992–2006*.

Tracklisting
UK CD Single
- "Emergency On Planet Earth" - 3:34
- "Emergency On Planet Earth" (Extended Version) - 4:10
- "If I Like It, I Do It" (Acoustic Version) - 4:40
- "Revolution 1993" (Demo) - 10:20

Source (edited): "http://en.wikipedia.org/wiki/Emergency_on_Planet_Earth_(song)"

Feels Just Like It Should (Jamiroquai song)

"**Feels Just Like It Should**" is the first single from British Acid Jazz band Jamiroquai's sixth studio album, *Dynamite*. The song was produced by Mike Spencer and Jay Kay. The track incorporates a bass line created by Kay as a human beatbox, a sample of which was first created during the recording of the band's 2001 album, *A Funk Odyssey*. The song was their fourth #1 on the U.S. Dance Chart and peaked at #8 on the UK Singles Chart.

Background
This track has been used by the BBC's advertising for the 2005 Children in Need appeal, which features Terry Wogan breakdancing to the song, was included in the computer game *FIFA 06*, and was featured in *Need for Speed: Most Wanted* as a remix by Timo Maas. It has also been used in a Cingular Music and Payless ShoeSource advertisement, and is available as a playable song in the Xbox 360 game, *Dance Dance Revolution Universe*. It was also used during a game montage for the Xbox 360 during E3 2006. The song was also recently used in 2010 during commercials for PlayStation Move and the HBO series *Hung*.

Tracklisting
UK CD1 (675968 1)
- "Feels Just Like It Should" – 4:34
- "Feels So Good" (Knee Deep Remix) – 3:44

UK CD2 (675968 2)
- "Feels Just Like It Should" – 4:34
- "Feels Just Like It Should" (Mark Ronson Remix) – 3:49
- "Feels Just Like It Should" (Timo Maas Remix) – 9:31

Source (edited): "http://en.wikipedia.org/wiki/Feels_Just_Like_It_Should_(Jamiroquai_song)"

Half the Man (Jamiroquai song)

"**Half The Man**" is the second single from British Acid Jazz group Jamiroquai's second studio album, *The Return of the Space Cowboy*. The track became the group's best-selling single to that point, peaking at #7 on the UK Singles Chart. The song was featured on the soundtrack of cult British surf movie *Blue Juice*. The song gained recognition for its popular B-Side, "Space Clav", which has never been included on any other Jamiroquai release. It is one of only four singles that does not appear on the group's greatest hits record.

Track listing
UK CD1
- "Half The Man" (Edit) – 3:35
- "Space Clav" – 4:56
- "Emergency On Planet Earth" (London Rican Mix) – 7:10
- "Half The Man" (Album Version) - 4:48

UK CD2
- "Half The Man" (Edit) - 3:35
- "When You Gonna Learn (Didgeridoo)" - 3:48
- "Too Young To Die" (Edit) - 3:22
- "Blow Your Mind" (Edit) - 3:51

Source (edited): "http://en.wikipedia.org/wiki/Half_the_Man_(Jamiroquai_song)"

High Times (song)

"**High Times**" is the fourth and final single from British Acid Jazz band Jamiroquai's third studio album, *Travelling Without Moving*. The song peaked at #3 on the UK Singles Chart.

Background
The song was written by Jason Kay. The song begins with the quote "You don't need a name in bright lights, you're a rock star. In some tinfoil, with a glass pipe, is your guitar." This refers

to cocaine. Both cocaine, and many other drugs are referenced in the song, all in a negative light, but it is jet lag the main reference during the chorus, "Last night, turned to daylight and a minute became a day", a desynchronosis that is often caused when travelling around the world during the tours. The radio edit of the song is widely ridiculed among fan circles for it's poor editing. There are some abrupt cuts in the song, and some words are cut out in an odd manner, such as the word "this" from the "This twisted, crystal kingdom" line. The Radio Edit was featured on the group's greatest hits compilation, High Times: Singles 1992-2006. This cut reached #14 in the UK Singles Chart. Some releases of *Travelling Without Moving* include a version of the song without the sample "Last Night Changed It All" as sung by Esther Williams and written by Joe Wheeler.

Tracklisting
UK CD1 (665370 2)
- "High Times" (Radio Edit) – 4:08
- "High Times" (Bionic Supachronic Mix) – 8:38
- "High Times" (Doobie Dub) – 6:46
- "High Times" (Album Version) – 5:57

UK CD2 (665370 5)
- "High Times (Radio Edit) – 4:08
- "High Times (Jamiroquai Mix) – 4:00
- "High Times (Jamiroquai Dub) – 5:30
- "High Times (Sanchez Radio Edit) – 4:02

UK 12" (665370 6)
- "High Times" (Bionic Supachronic Mix) – 8:38
- "High Times" (Jamiroquai Mix) – 4:00
- "High Times" (Doobie Dub) – 6:46
- "High Times" (Jamiroquai Dub) – 5:30

Music video
The music video for this song is filmed like a documentary with an inexpensive digital camera by the band manager of the band during the Latin American tour. In the video, the group is shown landing in a city airport, happy and excited. The remainder of the video shows candid scenes of Jamiroquai laughing at jokes, television, and having general fun. Chilean fans appreciated this music video for lead singer Jay Kay's cultural jacket throughout the video. However, the last few seconds were censored in some countries due to the usage of marijuana. An interesting fact about the video is that it can be seen as a polar opposite to *Virtual Insanity* in several ways - "Virtual Insanity" was the first single to be released from the album. This song was the last. Virtual Insanity was *Travelling's* most successful single, and its respective video was shot professionally, in contrast to "High Times", which was the album's least successful single, accompanied by an amateur video.

Source (edited): "http://en.wikipedia.org/wiki/High_Times_(song)"

Just Another Story

Just Another Story is a song by British band Jamiroquai. It is the opening track to the second Jamiroquai album *The Return of the Space Cowboy*, in all countries other than the U.S., where the song switches place with "Space Cowboy" to become the eleventh track. "Just Another Story" is the second longest album track by Jamiroquai next to "Revolution 1993" (however remixes and live performances of various other songs do exist).

Themes
The song deals with the problem of vigilantes who enforce justice by themselves, often harming innocents in the process. The main character, as described in the second verse, holds a gun to a minor's head, who apparently is both a drug dealer and a drug (ab)user. The "'94 tour" version holds alternative lyrics to the song which expand more on the whole theme.

"Just Another Story" is the only Jamiroquai track to feature the word "fucking" in the lyrics. In context the line is as follows:
"All these gangster kids are gettin' up-tight!
I gotcha! I gotcha where I want ya now! Nobody make a fucking move!"
The song is often cited by fans to be somewhat autobiographic to Jason Kay, the lead singer, who was homeless at a time and had committed criminal acts to survive.

The Return of the Space Cowboy has no parental advisory or sensory restriction placed on it despite the content of the song, although a DualDisc release of the band's sixth album *Dynamite* does feature a "behind the scenes" feature regarding the album's production. The documentary in which the same word was uttered was given a parental advisory sticker.

Song structure
Being nearly 9 minutes long, JAS is a song of a somewhat progressive nature. The song structure is as follows:
- Overture;
- Verse (x2);
- Outroduction.

The introduction to the song is appx. 2 minutes long, and can be considered to be an overture to the album. The introduction is sometimes seen (but was never officially released) as a separate song. The overture/introduction contains only one verse. The main part of the song has the second verse sung twice. The outroduction immediately follows the verses, and changes the mood of the song by inducing heavy wind instrumentation.

Some live versions (e.g. Paradiso '94) changed the structure of the song into this order:
- Verse #2 (x2);
- Outroduction;
- Overture
- (segue into next song).

Some other live versions had alternative

lyrics .

Mixes
- Album version - 8:45;
  - 1994 alternative lyrics version;
  - A pirate release of the album adds a gunshot at the end of the track. The gunshot stems from the ending of a different song called "D.S.", which was written by Michael Jackson and released on his 2CD compilation album, *HIStory: Past, Present and Future, Book I*.
- Unofficial instrumental mix - 8:45.

Source (edited): "http://en.wikipedia.org/wiki/Just_Another_Story"

Kids (Jamiroquai song)

"**The Kids**" is the fifth and final single from British Acid Jazz band Jamiroquai's second studio album, *The Return of the Space Cowboy*. The song failed to chart on the UK Singles Chart.

Background

It is commonly known amongst fanss that "The Kids" was written and performed during the 1993 Emergency on Planet Earth tour. It may either have been an outtake, or simply a song written after the album was fully produced and released. The live versions played during the tour had a different chorus when compared to the album version. After "The Kids" was recorded with previous drummer, Nick Van Gelder, Derrick McKenzie replaced Nick and all tracks from the Space Cowboy recording sessions were re-recorded with McKenzie on drums, aside from "The Kids", on which van Gelder's drumming remains. The song was probably left to be as it was because of time constraints related to the mastering process, production and release. "The Kids" is a song that deals with the rights of children and their social status in the world. The song is written to be absurdly loud and high in tempo, to possibly represent the immaturity of children, and more generally the whole early childhood of a person, which is usually a carefree time of life.

Tracklisting

UK CD Single
- "The Kids" - 4:13
- "When You Gonna Learn" (Live At Leadmill, Sheffield) - 9:51
- "When You Gonna Learn" (Digeridoo Instrumental) - 6:31

Source (edited): "http://en.wikipedia.org/wiki/Kids_(Jamiroquai_song)"

King for a Day (Jamiroquai song)

"**King For A Day**" is the fourth and final single from British Acid Jazz band Jamiroquai's fourth studio album, *Synkronized*. The song was written by Jay Kay. The song is a tribute to bassist Stuart Zender, who left the band shortly before *Synkronized* was completed. Jay Kay subsequently rerecorded all the songs on the album without Zender, and added "King For A Day" as the final track on the album. The song reached #20 on the UK Singles Chart. The single is renowned for being the first Jamiroquai single not only to include a remix of a non-single, but to include an enhanced element as well.

Track listing

UK CD1 (667973 2)
- "King For A Day" – 3:38
- "Planet Home" (Trabant Brothers Inc. Remix) – 7:20
- "Supersonic" (Dirty Rotten Scoundrels Ace Klub Mix) – 6:58

UK CD2 (667973 5)
- "King For A Day" – 3:38
- "Canned Heat" (Shanks & Bigfoot Extended Master Mix) – 6:29
- "Supersonic" (Radio Edit) – 3:40
- "Supersonic" (Video) – 3:56

Source (edited): "http://en.wikipedia.org/wiki/King_for_a_Day_(Jamiroquai_song)"

Lifeline (Jamiroquai song)

"**Lifeline**" is the third single from British acid jazz group Jamiroquai's studio album, *Rock Dust Light Star*. The single was released via Digital Download on January 24 2011. The song was written by band frontman Jay Kay and Matt Johnson. It is the band's third single to be released under Mercury Records. The single will not receive an official physical release. It appears that the Jamiroquai logo typeface has been stretched vertically for this release. The video for the single was made available on the group's YouTube account on January 7, 2011. The track has so far peaked at #99 on the UK Singles Chart. All three singles from Rock Dust Light Star have identical cover artwork, with the exception of the song title, which is printed in a different colour each time.

Tracklisting

Digital Download and CD Single
- "Lifeline" - 3:34

Promotional CD Single
- "Lifeline" - 3:34
- "Lifeline" (Fred Falke Remix) - 8:12
- "Lifeline" (Buzz Junkies Remix) - 9:08
- "Lifeline" (Alan Braxe Remix) - 5:46
- "Lifeline" (Pirupa Deadline Remix) - 3:57
- "Lifeline" (Pirupa Deadline Vocal) - 5:56

Music video

The music video features black and white footage of the band's Rock Dust Light Star tour, intertwined with footage of Jason performing the song. The video also features footage of the group meeting fans, staying in a hotel and performing the song on various television music programmes.

Source (edited): "http://en.wikipedia.org/wiki/Lifeline_(Jamiroquai_song)"

Light Years (Jamiroquai song)

"**Light Years**" is the fourth single from British Acid Jazz band Jamiroquai's second studio album, *The Return of the Space Cowboy*. The song peaked at #36 on the UK Singles Chart due to poor promotion of the track. In the US, the song hit #6 on the U.S. Dance Chart. The American version of the single features three mixes of the song by David Morales. The American album release features a live version of Light Years, performed in Merseille in December 1994, as a bonus track. Two main versions of the song exist: a Radio Edit, running at 3:59, and an album version, which lasts for 5:53.

Tracklisting

UK CD Single
- "Light Years" (Edit) – 3:59
- "Scam" (Live) – 5:13
- "Journey To Arnhemland" (Live) – 5:39
- "We Gettin' Down" (Live) – 9:31

US CD Single
- "Light Years" (Album Version) - 5:53
- "Light Years" (4 To Da Floor Mix) - 5:20
- "Light Years" (True Power Mix) - 7:50
- "Light Years" (Way Gone Mix) - 7:30
- "Half The Man" (Album Version) - 4:48

Source (edited): "http://en.wikipedia.org/wiki/Light_Years_(Jamiroquai_song)"

List of Jamiroquai songs

This list comprises all songs released and unreleased by British band Jamiroquai.

Source (edited): "http://en.wikipedia.org/wiki/List_of_Jamiroquai_songs"

Little L

"**Little L**" is the lead single from British acid jazz band Jamiroquai's fifth studio album, *A Funk Odyssey*. The song peaked at #5 on the UK Singles Chart. The song was written by Jay Kay, and was inspired by the breakup between himself and Denise van Outen, his former girlfriend, over his cocaine problem. The song was featured in the film *The Sweetest Thing*. A cover of the song is featured in the game Dance Dance Revolution Hottest Party.

Track listing

UK CD (671718 2)
- "Little L" (single edit) – 3:57
- "Little L (Wounded Buffalo Remix) – 5:08
- "Little L (Bob Sinclar Remix) – 5:35
- "Little L (Boris Dlugosch Remix) – 5:16
- "Little L" video – 3:57

UK cassette (671718 4)
- "Little L" (single edit) – 3:57
- "Little L" (Wounded Buffalo Remix) – 6:42

UK 12" (671718 6)
- "Little L" (single edit) – 3:57
- "Little L" (Wounded Buffalo Remix) – 6:41
- "Little L" (Bob Sinclar Remix) – 7:27
- "Little L" (Boris Dlugosch Remix) – 6:10

Source (edited): "http://en.wikipedia.org/wiki/Little_L"

Love Foolosophy

"**Love Foolosophy**" is the third single from British Acid Jazz band Jamiroquai's fifth studio album, *A Funk Odyssey*. The song was written by Jason Kay. The song's title is a play on words, using a makeshift homonym for "Philosophy" to imply that the singer is a fool for love, as it were. The song peaked at #14 on the UK Singles Chart.

The music video of the song features Heidi Klum. This song was also used in the credits for the unaired English pilot for Code Lyoko.

Tracklisting

UK CD1
- "Love Foolosophy"
- "Love Foolosophy" (Knee Deep Remix)
- "Love Foolosophy" (Bini + Martini Ocean Remix)
- "Love Foolosophy" (Video)

UK CD2
- "Love Foolosophy"
- "Love Foolosophy" (Twin Club Remix)
- "Little L" (Blaze Remix)

- "Love Foolosophy" (Alternative Video)

DVD Single
- "Love Foolosophy" (Video)
- "Picture Of My Life" (Radio 1 Acoustic Session) (Audio)
- "Black Crow" (Radio 1 Acoustic Session) (Audio)
- "Little L" (Video Clip)
- "You Give Me Something" (Video Clip)
- "Alright" (Video Clip)
- "Space Cowboy" (Video Clip)

Source (edited): "http://en.wikipedia.org/wiki/Love_Foolosophy"

Manifest Destiny (Jamiroquai song)

"**Manifest Destiny**" is a Jamiroquai song from their second album *The Return of the Space Cowboy*. Featuring a soul-oriented acid jazz style, the song primarily includes piano, bass, percussion, drums and horns. It was performed long before the release of *The Return of the Space Cowboy*, during the *Emergency on Planet Earth* tour. Then titled "Let Me Believe", the song had different lyrics and arrangements, however it's still recognizable as the basslines and chord progressions were the same. There's only one known recording of this version, and it's on an early silver bootleg called "Songs for Manitu".

Theme

The song refers to the consequences that the expansion of United States across North America (Manifest Destiny) had on Native American tribes in the 19th century.

Source (edited): "http://en.wikipedia.org/wiki/Manifest_Destiny_(Jamiroquai_song)"

Runaway (Jamiroquai song)

"**Runaway**" is the first and only single taken from British Acid Jazz band Jamiroquai's greatest hits compilation, *High Times: Singles 1992–2006*. The single was released on October 30, 2006. It was their fifth #1 on the U.S. Dance Chart and peaked at #18 on the UK Singles Chart.

Background

The song's lyrics relate to a protest regarding the group's record label, Sony BMG, who wanted to cut the band off after six records, however, their contract claimed they had an eight-record deal. Jay Kay confirmed this following a performance of the song in London's Jazz Cafe in August 2008. The single peaked at #18 on the UK Singles Chart. The promotional version of the single includes an early demo version of the song, which runs at 3:29, rather than the finished version of the song, which runs at 3:45.

Tracklisting
UK CD1
- "Runaway" (Jason Kay, Robert Harris, Matthew Johnson) – 3:44
- "Runaway" (Tom Belton Remix - Edit) – 3:30

UK CD2
- "Runaway" (Jason Kay, Robert Harris, Matthew Johnson) – 3:44
- "Runaway" (Tom Belton Remix) – 7:11
- "Runaway" (Grant Nelson Remix) – 6:10
- "Runaway" (Alan Braxe & Fred Falke Remix) – 6:37

UK 12" Single
- "Runaway" (Jason Kay, Robert Harris, Matthew Johnson) – 3:44
- "Runaway" (Grant Nelson Remix) – 6:10
- "Runaway" (Alan Braxe & Fred Falke Remix) – 6:37

UK Promotional Single
- "Runaway" (Demo Version) - 3:29

Source (edited): "http://en.wikipedia.org/wiki/Runaway_(Jamiroquai_song)"

Scam (Jamiroquai song)

"**Scam**" is a song by the British band Jamiroquai. The song appeared on the band's second album, *The Return of the Space Cowboy*. It is most often cited by fans as one of the most powerful protest songs by the band. Live performances of the song during the *The Return of the Space Cowboy* tour usually began with a lengthy trumpet solo, and have placed the song at the end of a long chain of songs segued into one another (most often in the order "Blow Your Mind", "Light Years", "Who the Funk Do You Think You Are?", "Emergency on Planet Earth", "Scam"). During the following tours, the song was mostly standalone. A "smooth remix" of the song was planned for a cancelled remix album called *Interpretations from Beyond*, which was scheduled to be released after *Travelling Without Moving*.

Composition and production

The song was created by merging two live-only Jamiroquai songs from the *Emergency on Planet Earth* era, "Do That Dance" and "Life Goes on" into one. Many elements were taken from both of the songs, such as the horn/trumpet line from the chorus of "Life Goes On", and some chord progressions from "Do That Dance". The album version of the song took heavy damage in terms of sound fidelity, as it was reduced to an "early radio"-like quality.

Theme

The song centres on fraud, the ones who commit it and the ones who are its victims. The song's protagonist tells a story of how he has to "Scam - that's the way to stay alive", because he himself was a victim of a one, as heard in a verse ("See, I had to lose my car, job, wife, dog, and home,/debts and threats on the telephone"). However, it also tells how politicians also lie to their people, giving false promises, and abusing their own powers.

Source (edited): "http://en.wikipedia.org/wiki/Scam_(Jamiroquai_song)"

Seven Days in Sunny June

"**Seven Days In Sunny June**" is the second single from British Acid Jazz band Jamiroquai's sixth studio album, *Dynamite*. Written by lead singer Jay Kay and new keyboardist Matt Johnson, the track is considered to be a throwback to the old acid jazz sound upon which Jamiroquai made its name. The song is, in effect, a tale of unrequited love. The song peaked at #14 on the UK Singles Chart. The song was also used in the soundtrack for the film *The Devil Wears Prada*.

Tracklisting

UK CD1
- "Seven Days In Sunny June" (Album Version) - 4:01
- "Seven Days In Sunny June" (Steve Mac Remix Radio Edit)

UK CD2
- "Seven Days In Sunny June" - 3:36
- "Seven Days In Sunny June" (Steve Mac Classic Remix)
- "Seven Days In Sunny June" (Oliver Lang Remix)
- "Seven Days In Sunny June" (Blackbeard Remix)

Source (edited): "http://en.wikipedia.org/wiki/Seven_Days_in_Sunny_June"

Soul Education

Soul Education is a song by Jamiroquai, the fourth track of their 1999 album, *Synkronized*. The song was written by Jay Kay and Toby Smith, and was issued as a promotional recording in France. No other release of this song is known to exist. This French, radio-only promo was released in very limited amounts, and is considered to be very rare today. The only track on the disc is a radio edit of the song, which is, interestingly, one second longer than its album version. The promo CD was released in a cardboard sleeve. The are two versions of the cover, which is simply a sticker. The first version is a rather colorful sticker, while the second one is a plain sticker, simply reading "JAMIROQUAI <<Soul Education>> 3:55". In live performances, the song is usually extended, sometimes lasting over 10 minutes, including additional verses, solos and so on.

Source (edited): "http://en.wikipedia.org/wiki/Soul_Education"

Space Cowboy (song)

"**Space Cowboy**" is the lead single from British band Jamiroquai's second studio album, *The Return of the Space Cowboy*. The single reached #17 in the UK Singles Chart and was their first #1 on the U.S. Dance Chart.

Background

Two very distinct versions of the song exist: One was recorded with Stuart Zender on bass, has a greater tempo, and uses a 'bass slap' technique during the chorus. This version is commonly known as the "Stoned Again Mix", even though it is the original version. The second version, the one that appears on the album is considerably different, with a lower tempo, and a completely dissimilar bassline. The bass on the album version was not played by Zender, but by an unknown artist only credited as "Mr. X" in the booklet. It was this song that earned Jason the "*space cowboy*" nickname in the British press. The U.S. version of the single contains remixes by David Morales. Most live versions of the song are very long, about 10–12 minutes, adding additional verses, and instrumental parts. While the album version utilizes no wind instruments, some live versions, such as the ones from the *Travelling Without Moving* era, or the *High Times: Singles 1992-2006* era, do. The version of the song played live is the "Stoned Again Mix".

Tracklisting

UK CD Single
- "Space Cowboy"
- "Journey To Arnhemland"
- "Kids"
- "Space Cowboy" (Demo Version)

US CD Single
- "Radio Edit"
- "Classic Radio Remix"
- "Album Version"
- "Classic Club Remix"
- "Instrumental"
- "Babinstrumental"

Official Versions
- Album Version
- Stoned Again Mix
- Radio Edit
- Classic Club Remix
- Classic Radio Remix
- Babinstrumental
- Instrumental
- Mayhem & Musaphia

Reconstruction Remix
- Demo Version
- Video Edit

Music video

A music video was shot for "Space Cowboy", using the "Stoned Again" Mix of the song. It was directed by Vaughan Arnell and mainly featured Jay Kay dancing around a blue room with multiple versions of him and the other band members appearing and disappearing. Occasional breaks show the band members against a blacklight with marijuana-leaf motifs. The video makes use of motion control photography to allow a seemingly-continuous shot as the camera pans around the room. The US video replaced the leaves with daisies, without Jay's consent. A video of the remix by David Morales also exists. "Space Cowboy" is a frequently covered song, with two notable cover versions; one by Jazzamor, and one by the band Jacarandaa.

Source (edited): "http://en.wikipedia.org/wiki/Space_Cowboy_(song)"

Stillness in Time

"**Stillness In Time**" is the third single from British Acid Jazz band Jamiroquai's second studio album, *The Return of the Space Cowboy*. The track peaked at #2 on the UK Singles Chart, making it the group's highest charting release to that date. The song was covered by Calvin Harris on the *Radio 1 Established 1967* collection, which was released in 2007. Three versions of the track exist: a Radio Edit, which runs at 3:43, the Album Version, which runs at 4:11, and the Vinyl Version, which runs at 6:13.

Tracklisting

UK CD1
- "Stillness In Time" (Radio Edit) – 3:40
- "Space Cowboy" (Classic Radio Edit) – 4:01
- "Space Cowboy" (Classic Club Mix) – 7:52
- "Stillness In Time" (Vinyl Version) – 6:13

UK CD2
- "Stillness In Time" (Vinyl Version) - 6:13
- "Emergency On Planet Earth" - 4:04
- "Space Cowboy" (Radio Edit) - 3:46
- "Light Years" (Radio Edit) - 3:59

Source (edited): "http://en.wikipedia.org/wiki/Stillness_in_Time"

Supersonic (Jamiroquai song)

"**Supersonic**" is the third single from British Acid Jazz band Jamiroquai's fourth studio album, *Synkronized*. The song was written by Jason Kay. The word "supersonic" is repeated a total number of 127 times throughout the song. The track was their third #1 on the U.S. Dance Chart and peaked at #3 on the UK Singles Chart. The single release features various remixes of the song. "Supersonic" was one of five tracks remixed in 2006 for the group's Classic Club releases.

Track listing

UK CD1 (667839 2)
- "Supersonic" (Radio Edit) – 3:40
- "Supersonic" (Pete Heller - The Love Mix) – 9:35
- "Supersonic" (Harvey's Fuel Altered Mix) – 6:35

UK CD2 (667839 5)
- "Supersonic" – 5:14
- "Supersonic" (Restless Soul Main Vocal) – 7:35
- "Supersonic" (Sharp Razor Remix) – 7:04

Music video

The music video begins with the message "ru ready for a supersonic synkronized audio and visual experience?" on the screen, flashing red. The camera zooms into an "orb" in the ? and Jay Kay appears. The orb moves around him while he is dancing the robot. The orb flashes along with the song's tune. A yellow one appears along with a green, orange and purple one. More orbs are seen behind the first five. The camera itself changes angle. The camera zooms into a red orb and Jay Kay is seen within it. The second part of the video features a tunnel-like stage with LED-covered walls. Jay Kay and other bandmembers are seen "hovering" across the stage, based on the film *Virtual Insanity*. The camera effects continue and a large audience appears. The LEDs form a sneaking man animation, possible homage to James Bond. Finally, the stage explodes and Jay Kay falls on the floor, the sneaking man LED animation is seen leaving from under him, stage right. He then says "You've been erased" and fires a rocket to the antagonist, creating a huge explosion.

Source (edited): "http://en.wikipedia.org/wiki/Supersonic_(Jamiroquai_song)"

Talullah (Shelter mixes)

"**Talullah (Shelter mixes)**" is a 12" White label house remix release by the British band Jamiroquai.

Track listing

Side A:
- Talullah (Shelter Vocal mix) - (??:??)

Side B:
- Talullah (Shelter dub) - (??:??)

Source (edited): "http://en.wikipedia.

Time Won't Wait

Time Won't Wait is a song by Jamiroquai, the final track of their 2005 album, *Dynamite*. The song was written by Jay Kay.

Source (edited): "http://en.wikipedia.org/wiki/Time_Won%27t_Wait"

Too Young to Die (Jamiroquai song)

"**Too Young To Die**" is the second single from British band Jamiroquai's debut studio album, *Emergency on Planet Earth*. The original version of the track runs at 10:18, however, both the single and album versions were cut, running at 3:22 and 6:05 respectively. The commercial single included all three versions of the track. The song's lyrics are about the fear of war and death due to political machinations. A music video was shot for "Too Young To Die". It was directed by W.I.Z., and consisted mainly of Jay Kay singing in what appears to be a desert military installation.

Artwork

The single's cover art depicts the lead singer, Jason Kay, in the background, looking into the camera, with a sky-blue "grill" of the Buffalo Man in the left, as hollow spots, which are slowly morphing into solid blue crosses, headstones, the polar opposites to the meaning of the buffalo man. This morphing happens as one moves his eyes from left to right over the cover of the single. There is also a banner near the bottom of the sleeve which has several images on it, including a picture of a baby with a caption beside it reading "Too Young To Die", an image of the mushroom cloud, and a Swastika, with the latter having a red "X" over it.

Tracklisting
UK CD Single
- "Too Young To Die" (Edit) - 3:22
- "Too Young To Die" (Extended Version) - 10:18
- "Too Young To Die" (Original) - 6:05
- "Too Young To Die" (Instrumental) - 6:22

Source (edited): "http://en.wikipedia.org/wiki/Too_Young_to_Die_(Jamiroquai_song)"

Virtual Insanity

"**Virtual Insanity**" is the lead single from British Acid Jazz band Jamiroquai's third studio album, *Travelling Without Moving*. The song reached #3 on the UK Singles Chart. The song also charted at #38 on the *Billboard* Modern Rock Tracks chart upon the single's release in America in 1997. In December 2010, the song was certified gold by the Recording Industry Association of Japan as a digital download to cellphones, five years after its release on the medium.

Music video

"Virtual Insanity" is perhaps Jamiroquai's best known music video. At the 1997 MTV Video Music Awards in September 1997, it earned ten nominations, winning four awards, including "Breakthrough Video" and the "Best Video of the Year." In 2006, it was voted 9th by MTV viewers in a poll on music videos that 'broke the rules.' It was directed by Jonathan Glazer. The single was released in the U.S. in 1997. At the 1997 MTV Video Music Awards, Jamiroquai performed the song, recreating the famous floor moving concept with two moving walkways on the stage floor, going in different directions, for Jay Kay to use to dance on.

Video description

Jay Kay in the "Virtual Insanity" music video

The video consists mainly of Jamiroquai's singer, Jay Kay, dancing and performing the song in a bright white room with a grey floor. Throughout the video, there are several combinations of couches and easy chair, which are the only furniture in the room. The video earned recognition from critics for its special effects: the floor appears to move while the rest of the room stays still. At some points the camera tilts up or down to show the floor or ceiling for a few seconds, and when it returns to the central position, the scene has completely changed. Other scenes show a crow flying across the room, a cockroach on the floor, the couches bleeding and the other members of Jamiroquai in a corridor being blown away by wind. This became the second video released by Jamiroquai to be successfully done in one complete, albeit composited, shot, *Space Cowboy* being the first. In a short making-of documentary, director Jonathan Glazer describes how the four walls move on a stationary grey floor with no detail, to give the illusion that the floor is moving. However, he does not state where the fourth wall is. In several shots, chairs or couches are fixed to the walls so that they appear to be standing still, when in fact they are moving. In other shots chairs remain stationary on the floor, but the illusion is such that they appear to be moving. The moving walls were not completely rigid and can be seen in some shots to wiggle slightly.

Trivia

The first 15 seconds of the album version of the song contain sampled sound effects from the beginning of the film *Alien*, when the "Mother" computer onboard the *Nostromo* spaceship receives an unidentified signal from a nearby planet. "Virtual Insanity" was covered by WaveGroup Sound for the 2005 Xbox game *Dance Dance Revolution ULTRAMIX 3* and the 2006 Konami PS2 game *Beatmania*, but a different cover version by Thomas Howard Lichtenstein has also appeared on many arcade versions of *DrumMania* and *Guitar Freaks*, also by Konami. It is also available in Konami's *Karaoke Revolution Volume 2* and *Lips* on some locales as downloadable content and in others as an on-disc song. In 1997, the song was used for a commercial for the 1997 MTV Video Music Awards, with Chris Rock parodying the video. It was also featured in the American Eagle Outfitters' Holiday 2006 in-store playlist. In 2007, the song was used in commercials to advertise *Space Week* on The Science Channel. In the same year, Blake Lewis performed the song on American Idol. On 27 December, 2009, Sezairi Sezali sang this song in the finals of the third season of Singapore Idol, on the same night he won Idol.

Single Information

The first B-side of the single is the song "Do You Know Where You're Coming From", which features M-Beat. It was released as a single earlier in 1996. The second B-side of the single, "Bullet", is probably one of the most mysterious Jamiroquai tracks ever written. The song starts with a 3-second percussion intro, and switches into a longer, very claustrophobic introduction. During this part, very faint vocals can be heard in the background, while the melody progresses. The vocals remained shrouded in a veil of mystery, until recently, after a fan did some "research" on the song. The broken lyrics seem to have been printed out by accident in a misprint of the booklet of the band's second album, *The Return of the Space Cowboy*. It should also be noted that the musical structure of the "long intro" to "Bullet" bears very heavy resemblance to the one of "Just Another Story", from *The Return of the Space Cowboy* and it could be a possible faint remix of Just Another Story or a faint sample of Just Another Story.

Tracklisting

UK CD1 (663613 2)
- "Virtual Insanity" – 4:04
- "Do You Know Where You're Coming From?" (Original Mix) – 4:59
- "Bullet" – 4:19
- "Virtual Insanity" (Album Version) – 5:40

UK CD2 (663613 5)
- "Virtual Insanity" – 4:04
- "Space Cowboy" (Classic Radio) – 4:01
- "Emergency On Planet Earth" (London Rican Mix) – 7:10
- "Do You Know Where You're Coming From" – 4:59

Cassette (663613 4)
- "Virtual Insanity" – 4:04
- "Virtual Insanity" (Album Version) – 5:40
- "Virtual Insanity" (Unreality Mix) – 3:54

Source (edited): "http://en.wikipedia.org/wiki/Virtual_Insanity"

When You Gonna Learn

"**When You Gonna Learn**" is the debut single by the British Acid Jazz band Jamiroquai. In the United Kingdom, the song is renowned for drawing attention to the band. It was originally released in 1992 by Acid Jazz Records, and later re-released on Sony Records in 1993 as the lead single from the *Emergency on Planet Earth* album. The lyric themes, like many of Jamiroquai's early songs, speak of environmental awareness. While the single commercially flopped, due to the lack of promotion, the song still remains well-known among fan circles, while its respective single, especially the Acid Jazz Records release, is a rare collectible, also valued much among fan circles.

History

The oldest demo tape of the song dates back to 1989. The only known demo version, unlike the album one, has a different chorus, and a largely different feeling to itself. The demo was recorded without Wallis Buchanan, as he probably wasn't a member of the band at that point. The demo version described here can only be found on the long-gone single for the track. It is labeled as the "Original Demo", what has led fans to consider the chance of more demo tapes being in existence, possibly in the possession of the guitarist of The Brand New Heavies who worked with the band at that time. While the most commonly known version of the song lasts for 3:50, and can be found on the CD album, another, longer version exists. It is known as the "J.K. mix" and lasts for 6 minutes and 28 seconds, and even then fading out in the ending. Fans often assume that the song's actual take might've been 10 or more minutes long, and was cut down because of lack of space. *When You Gonna Learn* was performed a great number of times during the band's tours. The song can be found on a silver bootleg called "Songs For Manitu". During the Emergency on Planet Earth, and the The Return of the

Space Cowboy tours, the song had a very lengthy didgeridoo introduction, as seen above, which almost always overshadowed the rest of the song in length. There are many versions of the song, with the most notable being the 30-minute performance in Amsterdam in 1994, which actually consists of multiple songs seguing seamlessly into one another.

Music video

A music video was shot for "When You Gonna Learn". It was directed by Morgan Lawley and interspersed artistic shots of lead singer Jay Kay, footage of the band playing and graphic stock footage of animals being experimented on and whaling operations. The original version was banned from MTV because of this imagery, and was replaced with a "cleaner" edit. The uncut video can be viewed on YouTube. When Jason talked about the video in an interview he said that his intention was to make an intense 'shock video' in the first place, depicting various experiments done on animals, whaling operations, and the Nazis, all in the most negative light: "I remember I did the video in America, and I remember the video got banned - you know the video got banned. Well, because I just went to Greenpeace and just took loads of footage of stuff... Stuf I just didn't think was right. So they said to me "We can't play that, it's got the Nazi party in there -- we can't play that".

Track listing

1992 (Acid Jazz Records)
CD Single
- "When You Gonna Learn" (Digeridoo) – 3:47
- "When You Gonna Learn" (Digeridon't) – 3:55
- "When You Gonna Learn" (JK Extended Mix) – 6:20
- "When You Gonna Learn" (Canté Hondo Mix) – 5:47
- "When You Gonna Learn" (Original Demo) – 4:50
- "When You Gonna Learn" (Canté Hondo Instrumental) – 5:47

12" Vinyl
- "When You Gonna Learn" (JK Extended Mix) – 6:20
- "When You Gonna Learn" (JK Instrumental) – 6:20
- "When You Gonna Learn" (Canté Hondo Mix) – 5:47
- "When You Gonna Learn" (Original Demo) – 4:50
- "When You Gonna Learn" (Digeridoo Instrumental) – 6:28

7" Vinyl
- "When You Gonna Learn" (Digeridoo) – 3:47
- "When You Gonna Learn" (Digeridon't) – 3:55

1993 (Sony Soho Square)
CD Single
- "When You Gonna Learn" (Digeridoo) – 3:47
- "Didgin' Out" (Live at the Milky Way, Amsterdam) – 3:27
- "Too Young to Die" (Live at Leadmill, Sheffield) – 5:25
- "When You Gonna Learn" (Canté Hondo Mix) – 5:47

Cassette Single
- "When You Gonna Learn" (Digeridoo) – 3:47
- "Didgin' Out" (Live at the Milky Way, Amsterdam) – 3:27

12" Vinyl
- "When You Gonna Learn" (JK Extended Mix) – 6:20
- "When You Gonna Learn" (JK Instrumental) – 6:20
- "When You Gonna Learn" (Live at Leadmill, Sheffield) – 9:50
- "When You Gonna Learn" (Canté Hondo Mix) – 5:47
- "When You Gonna Learn" (Original Demo) – 4:50
- "When You Gonna Learn" (Digeridoo Instrumental) – 6:28

7" Vinyl
- "When You Gonna Learn" (JK Extended Mix) – 6:20
- "When You Gonna Learn" (Canté Hondo Mix) – 5:47

Australian CD Single and US 12" Vinyl
- "When You Gonna Learn" (Digeridoo) – 3:47
- "When You Gonna Learn" (Digeridon't) – 3:55
- "When You Gonna Learn" (JK Extended Mix) – 6:20
- "When You Gonna Learn" (Canté Hondo Mix) – 5:47
- "When You Gonna Learn" (Original Demo) – 4:50
- "When You Gonna Learn" (Digeridoo Instrumental) – 6:28

US CD Single
- "When You Gonna Learn" (Digeridoo Edit) – 2:57
- "When You Gonna Learn" (Digeridon't Edit) – 3:01

Japanese CD Single
- "When You Gonna Learn" (Digeridoo) – 3:47
- "Too Young To Die" (7" Edit) – 3"22
- "When You Gonna Learn" (Canté Hondo Mix) – 5:47
- "Too Young To Die" (12" Version) – 6:04

Spanish CD Single
- "When You Gonna Learn" (Digeridoo) – 3:47
- "When You Gonna Learn" (JK Extended Mix) – 6:20

Contrary to the popular opinion, "When You Gonna Learn" is not the first single written and issued by Jason Kay, though it is the first single issued by his band. Jason's first single is a white label acetate called "Natural Energy", which was pressed only in 3 copies. Kiss 100 FM was the first radio station to play the single. The chord progressions of the song bearsstriking resemblance to the chord progressions of a Johnny "Hammond" Smith's song called "Los Conquistadores Chocolates", however, not by accident, because the booklet of the Acid Jazz Records release of the single bears a "special thanks" note to Smith, who gave permission to Jason to use the composition's structure. However, it is unknown whether Hammond received any royalties or not. The chord progressions of the Cantè hondo mix of this song bear even more resemblance to "Los conquistadores Chocolates". The Cantè Hondo mixes also uses the wind sound effect from Hammond's song. The cover used by Acid Jazz Records is completely different from the cover on Sony's release, even though a Spanish promo issued by Sony bears the AJ cover. There have been legal disputes between Acid Jazz Records and Epic Records because Epic re-released the single without Acid Jazz Records' consent.

Source (edited): "http://en.wikipedia.org/wiki/When_You_Gonna_Learn"

White Knuckle Ride

"**White Knuckle Ride**" is the first single from British alternative group Jamiroquai's studio album, *Rock Dust Light Star*. The single was released via Digital Download on October 31, 2010, with a Limited Edition Vinyl release due to appear on January 1, 2011. The song was written by band frontman Jay Kay and Matt Johnson. It is the band's first record to be released under Mercury Records. The band's official website originally announced that the single would be released on October 11. The band describe "White Knuckle Ride" as "a hi-octane retrospective on Jay's career experiences - a cautionary tale equally applicable to anyone's life in these pressure cooker times." It appears that the Jamiroquai logo typeface has been stretched vertically for this release. The video for the single was made available on the group's YouTube account on September 25.

Tracklisting
Digital Download and CD Single
- "White Knuckle Ride" - 3:35

Promotional CD Single #1
- "White Knuckle Ride" (Radio Edit) - 3:26
- "White Knuckle Ride" (Seamus Haji Radio Edit) - 3:00
- "White Knuckle Ride" (Seamus Haji Remix) - 6:39
- "White Knuckle Ride" (Seamus Haji Instrumental) - 6:39
- "White Knuckle Ride" (Monarchy Remix) - 7:00
- "White Knuckle Ride" (Monarchy Dub) - 6:45
- "White Knuckle Ride" (Penguin Prison Remix) - 5:36
- "White Knuckle Ride" (Penguin Prison Instrumental) - 5:28

Promotional CD Single #2 and UK Limited Edition 12" Vinyl
- "White Knuckle Ride" (Alan Braxe Remix) - 6:16
- "White Knuckle Ride" (Monarchy Remix) - 7:00
- "White Knuckle Ride" (Monarchy Dub) - 6:45
- "White Knuckle Ride" (Penguin Prison Remix) - 5:36
- "White Knuckle Ride" (Penguin Prison Instrumental) - 5:28

Music Video
The music video shows Jay Kay pursuing a Porsche 911 Carrera along a winding desert road from a helicopter. After several unsuccessful attempts at losing its pursuer - including driving in wide circuits to raise a cloud of dust to blind Kay, and taking a detour down a tree-lined dirt road - the driver comes to a halt under a viaduct and escapes on foot. Kay arrives to find the car abandoned with no sign of the driver, whose face is never shown.

Live Performances
- The X Factor UK - October 31, 2010: Week 3 Results Show (Alongside Rihanna and Bon Jovi)
- The X Factor Australia - December 13, 2010: The Final

Source (edited): "http://en.wikipedia.org/wiki/White_Knuckle_Ride"

You Give Me Something (Jamiroquai song)

"**You Give Me Something**" is the second single from British Acid Jazz band Jamiroquai's fifth studio album, *A Funk Odyssey*. The song was written by Jason Kay. The song peaked at #16 on the UK Singles Chart. The song is inspired by disco and funk theme, as implied by the album's title itself, *A Funk Odyssey*. It is the group's first single to be released on the DVD Single format.

Track listing
CD
- "You Give Me Something" – 3:17

- "You Give Me Something" (Cosmos Deep Space Remix) – 5:23
- "You Give Me Something" (Full Intention Remix) – 2:58
- "You Give Me Something" (R'n'B Remix) – 3:59
- "You Give Me Something" (King Saki Remix) – 4:04
- "You Give Me Something" (video) - 3:25

Cassette
- "You Give Me Something" - 3:17
- "Do It Like We Used To Do" - 6:49

DVD (Only 20,000 copies produced)
- "You Give Me Something" (video)
- "Do It Like We Used To Do" (audio)
- "Main Vein" (live) (audio)
- "Virtual Insanity" (video clip)
- "Cosmic Girl" (video clip)
- "Deeper Underground" (video clip)
- "Canned Heat" (video clip)

Source (edited): "http://en.wikipedia.org/wiki/You_Give_Me_Something_(Jamiroquai_song)"